g

SENTENCE CORRECTION

Verbal Preparation Guide

This essential guide takes the guesswork out of grammar by presenting every major grammatical principle and minor grammatical point tested on the GMAT. Don't be caught relying only on your ear; master the rules for correcting every GMAT sentence.

Sentence Correction GMAT Preparation Guide, 2007 Edition

10-digit International Standard Book Number: 0-9790175-7-2
13-digit International Standard Book Number: 978-0-9790175-7-5

Note: *GMAT, Graduate Management Admission Test, Graduate Management Admission Council,* and *GMAC* are all registered trademarks of the Graduate Management Admission Council which neither sponsors nor is affiliated in any way with this product.

8 GUIDE INSTRUCTIONAL SERIES

Math GMAT Preparation Guides

Number Properties (ISBN: 978-0-9790175-0-6)

Fractions, Decimals, & Percents (ISBN: 978-0-9790175-1-3)

Equations, Inequalities, & VIC's (ISBN: 978-0-9790175-2-0)

Word Translations (ISBN: 978-0-9790175-3-7)

Geometry (ISBN: 978-0-9790175-4-4)

Verbal GMAT Preparation Guides

Critical Reasoning (ISBN: 978-0-9790175-5-1)

Reading Comprehension (ISBN: 978-0-9790175-6-8)

Sentence Correction (ISBN: 978-0-9790175-7-5)

HOW OUR GMAT PREP BOOKS ARE DIFFERENT

One of our core beliefs at Manhattan GMAT is that a curriculum should be more than just a guidebook of tricks and tips. Scoring well on the GMAT requires a curriculum that builds true content knowledge and understanding. Skim through this guide and this is what you will see:

You will *not* find page after page of guessing techniques.

Instead, you will find a highly organized and structured guide that actually teaches you the content you need to know to do well on the GMAT.

You *will* find many more pages-per-topic than in all-in-one tomes.

Each chapter covers one specific topic area in-depth, explaining key concepts, detailing in-depth strategies, and building specific skills through Manhattan GMAT's *In-Action* problem sets (with comprehensive explanations). Why are there 8 guides? Each of the 8 books (5 Math, 3 Verbal) covers a major content area in extensive depth, allowing you to delve into each topic in great detail. In addition, you may purchase only those guides that pertain to those areas in which you need to improve.

This guide is challenging - it asks you to do more, not less.

It starts with the fundamental skills, but does not end there; it also includes the *most advanced content* that many other prep books ignore. As the average GMAT score required to gain admission to top business schools continues to rise, this guide, together with the 6 computer adaptive online practice exams and bonus question bank included with your purchase, provides test-takers with the depth and volume of advanced material essential for achieving the highest scores, given the GMAT's computer adaptive format.

This guide is ambitious - developing mastery is its goal.

Developed by Manhattan GMAT's staff of REAL teachers (all of whom have 99th percentile official GMAT scores), our ambitious curriculum seeks to provide test-takers of all levels with an in-depth and carefully tailored approach that enables our students to achieve mastery. If you are looking to learn more than just the "process of elimination" and if you want to develop skills, strategies, and a confident approach to any problem that you may see on the GMAT, then our sophisticated preparation guides are the tools to get you there.

HOW TO ACCESS YOUR ONLINE RESOURCES

Please read this entire page of information, all the way down to the bottom of the page! This page describes WHAT online resources are included with the purchase of this book and HOW to access these resources.

[**If you are a registered Manhattan GMAT student** and have received this book as part of your course materials, you have AUTOMATIC access to ALL of our online resources. This includes all simulated practice exams, question banks, and online updates to this book. To access these resources, follow the instructions in the Welcome Guide provided to you at the start of your program. Do NOT follow the instructions below.]

If you have purchased this book, your purchase includes 1 YEAR OF ONLINE ACCESS to the following:

> **6 Computer Adaptive Online Practice Exams**
>
> **Bonus Online Question Bank for SENTENCE CORRECTION**
>
> **Online Updates to the Content in this Book**

The 6 full-length computer adaptive practice exams included with the purchase of this book are delivered online using Manhattan GMAT's proprietary computer adaptive online test engine. The exams adapt to your ability level by drawing from a bank of more than 1200 unique questions of varying difficulty levels written by Manhattan GMAT's expert instructors, all of whom have scored in the 99th percentile on the Official GMAT. At the end of each exam you will receive a score, an analysis of your results, and the opportunity to review detailed explanations for each question. You may choose to take the exams timed or untimed.

The Bonus Online Question Bank for Sentence Correction consists of 25 extra practice questions (with detailed explanations) that test the variety of Sentence Correction concepts and skills covered in this book. These questions provide you with extra practice *beyond* the problem sets contained in this book. You may use our online timer to practice your pacing by setting time limits for each question in the bank.

The content presented in this book is updated periodically to ensure that it reflects the GMAT's most current trends. You may view all updates, including any known errors or changes, upon registering for online access.

Important Note: The 6 computer adaptive online exams included with the purchase of this book are the SAME exams that you receive upon purchasing ANY book in Manhattan GMAT's 8 Book Preparation Series. On the other hand, the Bonus Online Question Bank for SENTENCE CORRECTION is a unique resource that you receive ONLY with the purchase of this specific title.

To access the online resources listed above, you will need this book in front of you and you will need to register your information online. This book includes access to the above resources for ONE PERSON ONLY.

To register and start using your online resources, please go online to the following URL:

http://www.manhattangmat.com/access.cfm   (Double check that you have typed this in accurately!)

Your one-year of online access begins on the day that you register at the above URL. You only need to register your product ONCE at the above URL. To use your online resources any time AFTER you have completed the registration process, please login to the following URL:

http://www.manhattangmat.com/practicecenter.cfm

TABLE OF CONTENTS

g

Chapter 1
of
SENTENCE CORRECTION

INTRODUCTION:
THE 3 C's

In This Chapter . . .

THE 3 C's OF SENTENCE CORRECTION

Sentence Correction appears on the GMAT because business schools want reassurance that their admitted applicants grasp the 3 C's of good business writing:

1) Correctness
2) Concision
3) Clarity

Correctness refers to grammar: does the sentence adhere to the rules of Standard Written English ("SWE")? Much of the language that one hears in everyday speech actually violates one rule or another. The GMAT tests your ability to distinguish between good and bad grammar, even when the bad grammar seems natural.

For example: "Does everyone have their book?" This may sound fine, but only because you hear similar things all the time. The sentence actually violates the rules of SWE; it should be "Does everyone have his (or her) book?"

Concision refers to brevity: is the sentence written as economically as possible? The GMAT does not like to waste words. If an idea expressed in ten words can be expressed grammatically in eight, the GMAT prefers the eight.

Clarity refers to intelligibility: is the meaning of the sentence obvious and unambiguous? Confusing writing is bad writing. If you have to read a sentence more than once to figure out what the author is saying—or if the sentence lends itself to multiple interpretations—it is not a good sentence.

In this book, you will see examples of unclear, ambiguous sentences. You will learn to spot the type of imprecise language the GMAT tries to slip past you.

Correctness: A Closer Look

This book will steer you through the major points of SWE on the GMAT. Each chapter will present a major grammatical topic in depth and provide you with exercises to hone your skills in that topic. You'll learn the difference between what is truly grammatical and what just seems so by dint of familiarity.

This book presents you with the major grammatical issues tested on the exam: subject-verb agreement; verb tense, voice, and mood; pronouns; modifiers; parallelism; comparisons; and idioms. You will learn both the overarching principles of each grammatical topic and the nitty-gritty details that will help you differentiate correct grammar from poor grammar.

Grammatical *correctness* is the major focus of this book.

Even though a sentence may *sound* natural, it may not be grammatically correct according to the rules of Standard Written English.

Concision: A Closer Look

Almost every Sentence Correction problem will involve concision to some degree. Usually two or three of the wrong answers are wrong not only because they contain grammatical mistakes, but also because they are not written as succinctly as possible. If two choices are grammatically correct, but one is more concise than the other, then choose the shorter one.

Let's look at an example:

> Wordy: **Tom and his boss have differences over the way in which the company should invest its money.**
> Better: **Tom and his boss differ over how the company should make investments.**

The first sentence is easily understood, but still poorly written. The phrases **have differences**, **over the way in which**, and **invest its money** are all wordy. They can be replaced with more concise phrases, as in the second sentence.

Generally, the GMAT frowns upon using a phrase where a single word will do. For example, the phrase **have differences** means the same as the word **differ**, so why use the phrase?

Let's look at another example:

> Wordy: **Jane made an attempt not to see her new job as ideal.**
>
> Better: **Jane tried not to idealize her new job.**

Here, **made an attempt** and **to see ... as ideal** can be replaced by single words: **tried** and **idealize**.

Concision Continued: Avoid Redundancy

Another aspect of concision is redundancy. Each word in the correct choice must be necessary to the meaning of the sentence. If a word can be removed without distorting the meaning of the sentence, it is redundant and should be eliminated.

> Wordy: **Past experience reveals that cancer patients rarely ever exhibit the exact same symptoms.**
> Better: **Experience reveals that cancer patients rarely exhibit the same symptoms.**

The first sentence may seem fine at first glance, but it is poorly written. The word **past**, for example, is implicit in **experience** and can be eliminated. The words **ever** and **exact** are used only for emphasis (a practice the GMAT does not condone) and can be eliminated. Notice that the second version is more streamlined.

When stuck between two grammatically correct answer choices, choose the shorter one.

A common redundancy trap on the GMAT is the use of words with the same meaning:

Wordy: **The value of the stock rose by a 10% increase.**

Better: **The value of the stock increased by 10%.**   OR
The value of the stock rose by 10%.

Since **rose** and **increase** both imply growth, only one is needed to convey the correct meaning.

Wordy: **The three prices sum to a total of $11.56.**

Better: **The three prices sum to $11.56.**   OR
The three prices total $11.56.

Since **sum** and **total** convey the same meaning, only one is needed.

Wordy: **Being excited about her upcoming graduation, Kelsey could barely focus on her final exams.**

Better: **Excited about her upcoming graduation, Kelsey could barely focus on her final exams.**

Here, **being** does not add to the meaning of the sentence, so it should be eliminated. In fact, **being** almost always signals redundancy on the GMAT. You should avoid it whenever possible.

Can you find and locate the words in this sentence that are redundant? (Hint: Don't *look* too hard.)

Clarity: A Closer Look

Clarity is less common than correctness or concision as an issue in Sentence Correction. Generally, the meaning of GMAT sentences is clear the first time you read them. When clarity becomes an issue, it is usually because the original meaning (or intent) of the sentence has become warped in the answer choices. Thus, the original intent is no longer clear.

Your task in Sentence Correction is to correct grammar and style without changing the original meaning of the sentence. If an answer choice alters the original meaning, it is incorrect.

Most instances of *altered meaning* fall into one of four major categories:

1) **Word Placement**
2) **Known vs. Unknown**
3) **Multiple Meanings**
4) **"Such As" vs. "Like"**

the new standard

Clarity of Meaning: Word Placement

Beware of words that move from one position to another; the placement of a single word can alter the meaning of a sentence. For example:

> **All** the children are covered with mud.

> The children are **all** covered with mud.

In these sentences, changing the placement of **all** shifts the intent from the <u>number</u> of children covered with mud to the <u>extent</u> to which the children are covered with mud. Let's look at another example:

> **Only** the council votes on Thursdays.

> The council **only** votes on Thursdays.

> The council votes **only** on Thursdays.

Note that the meaning of the sentence changes as **only** shifts position:

In the first sentence, the placement of **only** indicates that the council alone votes on Thursdays (as opposed to the board, perhaps, which votes on Mondays and Fridays).

In the second sentence, the placement of **only** creates an ambiguity. One interpretation is that the council's sole activity on Thursdays is to vote (as opposed to Wednesdays, perhaps, when the council engages in several activities). The other, more common interpretation is that the council does not vote on any day but Thursday (as opposed to voting on Mondays or Tuesdays, for example).

In the third sentence, the placement of **only** indicates unambiguously that the council does not vote on any day but Thursday.

Consider this example:

> **Following** the rules will lead to success on the GMAT.
> The **following** rules will lead to success on the GMAT.

In this case, shifting the position of **following** changes the meaning of the sentence, because it changes the meaning of **following** itself. In the first sentence, **following** acts as a gerund (a verb acting as a noun), with the meaning "Adherence to the rules will lead to..." In the second sentence, however, **following** acts as an adjective, with the meaning "The rules listed below will lead to..."

If a word changes its position in the answer choices, you must consider whether the change has an impact on the meaning of the sentence. Look out especially for short "determiners" that count or otherwise restrict nouns (such as **only** and **all**).

Sometimes a change in the position of a single word can alter the meaning of an entire sentence.

Clarity of Meaning: Known vs. Unknown

This category includes those questions where the original sentence is certain about an outcome but the answer choices indicate uncertainty (or vice versa), or where the original sentence discusses a hypothetical situation but the answer choices present it as an actual situation (or vice versa).

A sentence that makes a declaration of certainty does not convey the same meaning as one that allows for doubt. For example:

> Certain: The sudden drop in interest rates **will** create more favorable investment opportunities.
>
> Uncertain: The sudden drop in interest rates **may** create more favorable investment opportunities.

In the first sentence, the use of **will** indicates the author's certainty: the outcome is guaranteed. In the second sentence, however, the use of **may** indicates the author's uncertainty: the outcome is possible but not guaranteed. Let's look at another example:

> Certain: The court ruled that the plaintiff **must** pay full damages.
>
> Uncertain: The court ruled that the plaintiff **should** pay full damages.

In the first sentence, the use of **must** indicates an absolute, legally binding obligation on the part of the plaintiff to pay the damages. In the second sentence, however, the use of **should** indicates a moral obligation only; the plaintiff is not bound to pay the damages. In this particular case, **should** cannot be correct since a court cannot impose a moral obligation on a plaintiff. The meaning of the sentence does not allow room for uncertainty.

When you see words of uncertainty (e.g. **may, might, should, ought, would, can, could**) in the answer choices, you must check whether the meaning of the original sentence requires doubt or certainty.

A related issue involves clarifying whether a sentence is describing an actual or a hypothetical situation. If the original sentence discusses a hypothetical situation, the correct answer choice cannot present the situation as fact (or vice versa). For example:

> Hypothetical: The colors of the sky **were as if** painted by a thousand angels.
>
> Actual: The colors of the sky **were** painted by a thousand angels.

The first sentence makes clear, through use of **as if**, that the sky was not really painted by angels. The second sentence, however, in dropping **as if**, turns the meaning from hypothetical to actual: the sky really was painted by angels.

> *A sentence that expresses certainty about an outcome should not be changed to express uncertainty about that outcome (and vice versa).*

Let's look at another example:

> Actual: If Chris and Jad met, they **discussed** mathematics.

> Hypothetical: If Chris and Jad met, they **would discuss** mathematics.

The first sentence could be the conclusion of a long debate in which it had been established as fact that Chris and Jad actually met: "If this did indeed happen, then this is the consequence." The second sentence, however, predicts the consequences of a hypothetical meeting of the two men: "If this were to happen, then this would be the consequence."

Be aware of whether the original sentence is actual or hypothetical, certain or uncertain.

Clarity of Meaning: Words with Multiple Meanings

Some words can be read in more than one way, altering the meaning of the sentence according to the given interpretation. Consider the following:

> The **light** fabric makes the shirt easy to fold.

> The shirt is easy to fold, and is very **light**.

The first sentence makes clear that **light** in this context means "not heavy." However, in the second sentence, **light** could mean either "pale" or "not heavy." The context does not establish the meaning clearly.

 If the precise meaning of a word cannot be determined from the context, look for an answer choice that provides a definite, fixed meaning.

Clarity of Meaning: "Such As" vs. "Like"

Such as is used to indicate examples. **Like** is used to indicate similarity. Contrast the following sentences:

> Animals **such as** lions and zebras live on the Serengeti Plain.

> Animals **like** lions and zebras live on the Serengeti Plain.

The first sentence indicates that lions and zebras are specific examples of animals that live on the Serengeti. The second sentence indicates only that animals *similar* to lions and zebras (tigers, perhaps?) live on the Serengeti, but it is not clear whether lions and zebras themselves actually do.

In correcting the grammar of a sentence, be sure that the original meaning of that sentence remains clear.

Problem Set

The underlined portion of each sentence below may contain one or more errors. Each sentence is followed by a bold-faced sample answer choice that changes the underlined portion in some way. However, in attempting to correct the original sentence, the bold-faced sample answer violates either the principle of CONCISION or CLARITY OF MEANING. Identify the specific error contained in each bold-faced fragment. Choose from among the following errors:

<u>CONCISION ERRORS:</u>
(1) WORDINESS
(2) REDUNDANCY

<u>CLARITY ERRORS:</u>
(1) WORD PLACEMENT
(2) KNOWN vs. UNKNOWN
(3) MULTIPLE MEANINGS
(4) "SUCH AS" vs. "LIKE"

1. <u>No matter how much voters may support environmental causes in public opinion polls,</u> when asked to vote for tax increases to fund environmental initiatives, many voters continue to vote with their pockets, not their consciences.
Even though voters support environmental causes in public opinion polls,

2. <u>After the fact that the test format was changed, scores decreased by more than 25%.</u>
After the changes were made in the test format, scores dropped by more than a 25% decrease.

3. <u>Once the two parties reached an agreement,</u> they began to work out the details of the settlement.
Once an agreement was reached by the two parties,

4. The farmer was angry when he learned that his neighbor's pigs would <u>no longer be kept in their pen.</u>
from then on be free.

5. She is the most dedicated gardener on the block, <u>every day watering the more than 50 plants and flowers in her yard.</u>
every day watering more than the 50 plants and flowers in her yard.

6. She was surprised that the new plant food did not cause her plants to grow taller, when she <u>had fully expected it to have the effect of increasing the size of the plants.</u>
had had the full expectation that the effect would have been present.

7. She had already opened the door <u>before when everyone had yelled,</u> "Surprise!"
before when everyone yelled,

8. Although his wife was nearly eighty when she died, he liked to remember her <u>as she was when they have first met.</u>
as though they had first met.

9.   After the renovations, the museum boasted a new atrium-style entrance, <u>to which having been added wood paneling and the artwork of several notable American painters.</u>
wood paneling and the artwork of several notable American painters having been added to it.

10.   Students are encouraged to pursue <u>extracurricular activities such as student government, sports, and the arts, these being a variety of activities from which students might choose.</u>
any of a variety of extracurricular activities like student government, sports, and the arts.

11.   Martin's routine includes <u>reading the daily newspaper and going over to the gym.</u>
reading the newspaper and going to the gym daily.

12.   Studies have shown a mentor to be a significant factor in <u>causing an increase of students' school academic performance.</u>
increasing a student's academic performance in school

13.   Students who elect majors in the sciences, <u>like those of computer programming, biochemistry, and physics,</u> can expect an average annual salary that is 50% higher than that of students majoring in the humanities.
such as those of computer programming, biochemistry, and physics

14.   It seems possible that the power outage <u>may have been caused by the lightning storm, having caused the storm.</u>
may have been caused by the lightning storm.

15.   Environmentalists warned that the drop in the pond's algae levels <u>so that they were the lowest in over a century were</u> the first sign of a serious ecological catastrophe.
to what would be the lowest in over a century was

1. **(Clarity) KNOWN vs. UNKNOWN:** The revised fragment is less wordy than the original sentence, but it also eliminates the word **may**. This changes the meaning of the original sentence from something uncertain to something certain.

2. **(Concision) REDUNDANCY:** The revised fragment makes the opening of the sentence less wordy. However, it is redundant to include both the words **dropped** and **decrease**.

3. **(Concision) WORDINESS:** Use of the passive voice makes the answer choice wordier and slightly awkward.

4. **(Clarity) MULTIPLE MEANINGS:** The original sentence makes clear that the farmer is upset at the thought of his neighbor's pigs roaming around at liberty. However, replacing the phrase **no longer be kept in their pen** with the phrase **from then on be free** muddies the meaning of the original sentence by allowing the possibility that the farmer is angry that his neighbor will no longer charge money for his pigs (perhaps both farmers raise pigs, and how can you compete with free pigs?). The two potential interpretations of the word **free**—either "at liberty" or "available for no charge"—make the meaning of the altered sentence unclear.

5. **(Clarity) WORD PLACEMENT:** Changing the placement of **the** in the sentence implies that she waters more than her own 50 plants and flowers, including plants and flowers that are not hers.

6. **(Concision) WORDINESS:** The original sentence is wordier than necessary; the new portion only makes it wordier. By replacing **had fully expected** with **had had the full expectation**, we only add more words and make the sentence needlessly confusing. A better choice might be: **had fully expected it to have this effect.**

7. **(Concision) REDUNDANCY:** The revised fragment correctly removes the word **had** from the second position in the original sentence. As we'll see in Verb Tense, we don't need **had** for the later past action. However, the original sentence also contains a redundancy error that the new portion does not repair. The corrected sentence should include *either* the word **before** or the word **when**. A better choice might be: **had already opened the door when everyone yelled.**

8. **(Clarity) KNOWN vs. UNKNOWN:** The revised fragment correctly replaces the word **have** with the word **had**. However, by replacing **as she was when** with **as though**, the new sentence suggests that the first meeting between the man and his wife was hypothetical (when, in fact, it was an actual event). A better choice might be: **as she was when they first met.**

9. **(Concision) WORDINESS:** The original sentence is wordy, but so is the revised fragment. The phrase **having been added to it** is very awkward. A better choice might be **to which wood paneling and the artwork of several notable American painters had been added.**

10. **(Clarity) "SUCH AS" vs. "LIKE":** The revised fragment is less wordy than the original sentence. However, in substituting the word **like** for the phrase **such as**, the revised fragment alters the intent of the original sentence. **Such as** is used to give examples, whereas **like** is used to make a comparison. The new sentence implies that student government, sports, and the arts are similar to extracurricular activities, when they actually are examples of extracurricular activities. A better choice might be: **any of a variety of extracurricular activities such as student government, sports, and the arts.**

11. **(Clarity) WORD PLACEMENT:** The revised fragment correctly removes the word **over** from the original sentence, making it less wordy. However, moving the word **daily** from before **newspaper** to after **gym** implies that Martin goes to the gym every day, something that is not stated explicitly in the original sentence.

12. **(Concision) REDUNDANCY:** The revised fragment nicely condenses the original wordy sentence. However, it still fails to address a redundancy issue: The word **academic** already conveys the concept of **in school**. A better choice might be: **increasing a student's academic performance.**

13. **(Concision) WORDINESS:** The revised fragment correctly employs the phrase **such as** to give examples of science majors. However, the phrase **those of** is not needed here. A better choice might be: **such as computer programming, biochemistry, and physics.**

14. **(Concision) REDUNDANCY:** The revised fragment eliminates some of the wordiness of the original sentence. However, the verb construction **may have been** is not necessary, since the word **possible** (from the beginning of the sentence) already conveys the element of uncertainty. A better choice might be: **was caused by the lightning storm.**

15. **(Clarity) KNOWN vs. UNKNOWN:** While the revised fragment correctly changes the final verb from **were** to **was**, its use of the verb construction **would be** implies that these levels are hypothetical, when in fact they are measurable and actual. A better choice might be: **to the lowest in over a century was.**

Sentence Correction

Now that you have completed your study of CONCISION & CLARITY, it is time to test your skills on problems that have actually appeared on real GMAT exams over the past several years.

The problem set that follows is composed of past GMAT problems from two books published by GMAC (Graduate Management Admission Council):

The Official Guide for GMAT Review, 11th *edition* (pages 638-660)
The Official Guide for GMAT Verbal Review (pages 234-253)

The problems in the set below are primarily focused on CONCISION & CLARITY issues. For each of these problems, identify errors in the answer choices relating to concision and clarity. Remember to avoid answer choices that are unnecessarily wordy or contain redundancies, and those that muddy the meaning or alter the intent of the original sentence.

Concision & Clarity

> *11*[th] *edition:* 8, 12, 14, 33, 36, 44, 80, 101, 118, 120, 124
> *Verbal Review:* 2, 22, 26, 43, 54, 69, 75, 87, 105, 109

Chapter 2
of
SENTENCE CORRECTION

SUBJECT-VERB
AGREEMENT

In This Chapter . . .

- Eliminate the Middleman
- "Of" is Just Another Middleman
- "And" vs. Additive
- "Or," "Either…Or," & "Neither…Nor"
- Collective Nouns are Singular
- Indefinite Pronouns: Usually Singular
- "Each" and "Every": Singular Sensations
- Numerical Words and Phrases
- A Subject Phrase: Singular Again
- When In Doubt, Think Singular
- Flip It!

SUBJECT-VERB AGREEMENT

Every sentence has a subject and a verb which must agree in number.

A singular subject requires a singular verb form:
The dog runs out of the house.

A plural subject requires a plural verb form:
The dogs run out of the house.

Singular and plural verb forms are second nature to you—you use them so often that there is nothing to memorize. Unfortunately, the writers of the GMAT know that your ear is close to perfect when it comes to matching a singular verb form to a singular subject and matching a plural verb form to a plural subject. Therefore, the GMAT tries to confuse you before you make that subject-verb match.

How? The GMAT tries to make the subject of each sentence as confusing as possible, so that you do not know whether the subject is singular or plural! If you do not know the number of the subject, then you will not be able to select a verb form that agrees with it. The key, then, to making subjects and verbs agree in GMAT sentences is to FIRST determine whether the subject of each sentence (or clause) is singular or plural.

> To find the simple subject, eliminate any modifiers.

Eliminate the Middleman

The most common way the GMAT confuses the number of the subject is to split up the subject and the verb by inserting a phrase in between. You must learn to eliminate the intervening phrase—the middleman—so that the true subject becomes clear.
For example:

The houses of that rich man (contain/contains) very expensive furniture.

What is the subject of this sentence: houses or man? Eliminate the middleman—the modifying phrase that separates the subject from the verb.

The houses ~~of that rich man~~ (contain/contains) very expensive furniture.

Now it is clear that the plural subject **houses** requires the plural verb form **contain**.

The houses of that rich man CONTAIN very expensive furniture.

"Of" is Just Another Middleman

Do not get confused by subjects followed by the word **of**. These "of" constructions are just clever middlemen that try to disguise the true subject. Just as with other middlemen, you should eliminate the "of" construction in order to find the true subject. For example:

> **The discovery of new lands (was/were) vital to the expansion of the British Empire.**

Eliminate the "of" construction to see that **discovery** is the true subject. As **discovery** is singular, it requires the singular verb form **was**.

> **The discovery ~~of new lands~~ WAS vital to the expansion of the British Empire.**

Another example:

> **The building of tall skyscrapers (has/have) increased in the past few years.**

Eliminate the "of" construction to see that **building** is the true subject. As **building** is singular, it requires the singular verb form **has**.

> **The building ~~of tall skyscrapers~~ HAS increased in the past few years.**

A final example:

> **The actions of my friend (is/are) not very wise.**

Eliminate the "of" construction to see that **actions** is the true subject. As **actions** is plural, it requires the plural verb form **are**.

> **The actions ~~of my friend~~ ARE not very wise.**

If you can remove a phrase from the sentence, and the sentence still makes sense, the phrase is likely a "middleman."

"And" vs. Additive

The word **and** can unite two or more singular subjects, forming a compound plural subject. For example:

> **Joe and his friends ARE going to the beach.**
> **Mathematics, history, and science ARE required high-school subjects.**

Notice that these compound subjects take a plural verb form (**are**).

There are other words or phrases besides **and** that can add to a subject. These are called additive phrases. Some examples include:

> **along with, in addition to, as well as, accompanied by, together with, including**

Unlike the word **and**, these additive phrases do not form compound subjects. Therefore, the number of the subject does not change as a result of the additive phrase. For example:

> **Joe, along with his friends, IS going to the beach.**
> **Mathematics, in addition to history and science, IS a required subject.**

Notice that the singular subjects (**Joe** and **Mathematics**) remain singular despite the additive phrases (**along with** and **in addition to**). Therefore, they require the singular verb form (**is**).

REMEMBER: Only the word **AND** can change a singular subject into a plural one. Singular subjects followed by additive phrases remain singular subjects.

An additive phrase is just another "middleman."

"Or," "Either . . . Or," & "Neither . . . Nor"

Some subjects contain disjunctive phrases such as "or," "either . . . or," & "neither . . . nor." In these sentences, there are two subjects. If one of the subjects is singular and the other subject is plural, what verb form should be used? The answer is simple: find the subject that is NEAREST to the verb and make sure that the verb agrees in number with this subject. For example:

> **Neither the coach nor the players ARE going to the beach.**
> **Neither the players nor the coach IS going to the beach.**

Notice that in both of these sentences, there are two subjects (**coach** and **players**) joined by a disjunctive phrase (**neither . . . nor**). In the first example, the plural subject **players** is nearest to the verb, so the verb takes the plural form **are**. In the second example, the singular subject **coach** is nearest to the verb, so the verb takes the singular form **is**.

(Note that when the words **either** or **neither** are in a sentence alone (without **or/nor**), they are not considered part of a disjunctive phrase. In these cases, they are considered singular and take only singular verbs.)

Collective Nouns are Singular

A collective noun is a noun that looks singular (it usually does not end with an "s") but refers to a group of people. Some examples include:

administration, army, audience, class, crowd, faculty, orchestra, team

Collective nouns are always considered singular and therefore require singular verb forms. For example:

> **The crowd IS cheering as the home team TAKES the field.**
> **Our army IS attacking the enemy.**

Each collective noun (**crowd**, **team**, & **army**) takes a singular verb form.

Indefinite Pronouns: Usually Singular

Pronouns are words that replace other nouns or pronouns. An indefinite pronoun is one that is not specific about the thing to which it refers. **Anyone** is an example of an indefinite pronoun. The following indefinite pronouns are considered singular subjects and therefore require singular verb forms. Note that all the pronouns that end in **-one**, **-body**, or **-thing** fall into this category.

SINGULAR PRONOUNS	
Anyone, Anybody, Anything	Someone, Somebody, Something
Everyone, Everybody, Everything	No one, Nobody, Nothing
Whatever, Whoever	Each, Every
Either*, Neither*	
(Either and neither may require a plural verb form when paired with or/nor.)	

There are, however, 5 indefinite pronouns which can be either singular or plural depending on the context of the sentence. You can remember these 5 by the word SANAM, which is composed of the first initial of each word.

THE SANAM PRONOUNS: **S**ome, **A**ny, **N**one, **A**ll, **M**ost

How can you tell if these pronouns are singular or plural? Look at the "of" construction which usually follows the pronoun. You may recall that you are generally supposed to ignore "of" constructions (as they are misleading middlemen). The SANAM pronouns are the exceptions to this rule: you should look at the object of the "of" construction to determine the number of the subject.

> **Some of the money WAS stolen from my wallet. (money** is singular)
> **Some of the documents WERE stolen from the bank. (documents** is plural)

the new standard

To determine subject-verb agreement, you must first decide whether the subject is singular or plural.

"Each" and "Every": Singular Sensations

You just learned that when **each** or **every** is the subject of a sentence, it requires a singular verb form. The same is true for any subject preceded by the word **each** or **every**:

> **Every dog HAS paws.**
> **Every dog and cat HAS paws.**
> **Each of these shirts IS pretty.**

One may mistake the subject of the second and third sentences to be plural. However, because the subject is preceded by **each** or **every**, it is considered singular and therefore requires a singular verb form. Note, however, that when **each** or **every** follows a subject, it has no bearing on the verb form. For example:

> **They each ARE great tennis players.**

Here, the plural subject **they** requires the plural verb form **are**.

Numerical Words and Phrases

The phrase **the number of** always takes a singular verb form.
The phrase **a number of** always takes a plural verb form.

> **The number of hardworking students in this class IS quite large.**
> **A number of students in this class ARE hard workers.**

Notice that both sentences focus on the word **students**. Yet in the first sentence the subject is singular, while in the second sentence the subject is plural.

Other numerical words—**majority**, **minority**, **plurality**—can be either singular or plural depending on their context. If one means the many individual parts of the totality, then use a plural verb form:

> **The majority of the students in this class ARE hard workers.**

If one means the totality itself, then use a singular verb form:

> **The student majority IS opposed to the death penalty.**

The numbers of is neither singular nor plural. It is simply incorrect. Never select an answer choice containing the phrase **the numbers of**.

A Subject Phrase: Singular Again

Sometimes the subject of a sentence is an entire phrase or clause. These subjects are always singular and require singular verb forms. For example:

> **Having good friends IS a wonderful thing.**
> **Whatever they want to do IS fine with me.**

Do not be confused by the fact that the subject phrase may contain plural words within it (**friends**). Remember that the entire phrase (**having good friends**) constitutes the subject, and all subject phrases are singular.

When In Doubt, Think Singular

You may have noticed that confusing subjects are more often singular than plural.

Singular subjects dominate the chart. Thus, if you cannot remember a particular rule for determining the number of a subject, place your bet that the subject is singular!

Singular Subjects	Plural Subjects	It Depends
A singular subject linked to other subjects by an additive phrase	Subjects joined by the word **and**	Subjects joined by disjunctive phrases
Collective nouns		
Most indefinite pronouns		SANAM pronouns
Subjects preceded by the words **each** or **every**		
Subjects preceded by the phrase **the number of**	Subjects preceded by the phrase **a number of**	Other numerical words
Subject phrases or clauses		

> Confusing subjects are more often singular than plural, and therefore they usually require singular verb forms.

Flip It!

In most English sentences the subject precedes the verb. However, the GMAT often attempts to confuse you by inverting this order and placing the subject after the verb. Remember that you must always find the subject first in order to determine if it is singular or plural; then you can select the appropriate verb form to agree in number. In sentences in which the subject follows the verb, flip the word order of the sentence so that the subject precedes the verb.

> Incorrect: **Near the office buildings SIT a lonely house, inhabited by squatters.**
>
> Flip it!:   **A lonely house, inhabited by squatters, SITS near the office buildings.**
>
> Correct: **Near the office buildings SITS a lonely house, inhabited by squatters.**

Notice that in the original sentence, the singular subject **house** follows the verb. The verb form **sit** is mistakenly plural, but your ear may not catch this error because it is near the plural word **buildings**. By flipping the subject **house** so that it precedes the verb, we see that it must take the singular form **sits**.

> Incorrect: **There IS a young man and an older woman at the bus stop.**
> Flip it!: **A young man and an older woman ARE at the bus stop.**
> Correct: **There ARE a young man and an older woman at the bus stop.**

By flipping the subject so that it precedes the verb, we can see that the subject **a young man and an older woman** is plural, and therefore requires the plural verb form **are**.

Note that the inverted verb-subject order is especially common in sentences that begin with the constructions **there is** and **there are**.

Problem Set

In each of the following 15 sentences (a) circle the verbs, (b) underline the subjects, and (c) determine whether each subject agrees in number with its corresponding verb. If the subject is singular, the verb form must be singular. If the subject is plural, the verb form must be plural. If there is an error in subject-verb agreement, (d) rewrite the sentence correcting the mistake. If the sentence is correct as it is, mark it with the word CORRECT.

1.   The traveling salesman was dismayed to learn that neither his sons nor his daughter were interested in moving.

2.   I was so thirsty that either of the two drinks were fine with me.

3.   A number of players on the team have improved since last season.

4.   Jack, along with some of his closest friends, is sharing a limo to the prom.

5.   The recent string of burglaries, in addition to poor building maintenance, have inspired the outspoken woman to call a tenants meeting.

6.   There is, according to my doctor, many courses of treatment available to me.

7.   The sun shining on the flowerbeds make a beautiful sight.

8.   The placement of the unusual artwork in the mansion's various rooms was impressive.

9.   Just around the corner is a bakery and a supermarket.

10.   Planting all these seeds is more involved than I thought.

11.   Whoever rented these movies has to take them back before midnight.

12.   Tired of practicing, the orchestra decide to walk out on their astonished conductor.

13.   The young bride, as well as her husband, were amazed by the generosity of the wedding guests.

14.   Neither she nor her parents understands the challenging math problem.

15.   A congressional majority is opposed to the current policy.

The following answer key only corrects errors in subject-verb agreement. You may have identified additional subjects and verbs that were already correct.

1.   The traveling salesman was dismayed to learn that neither his sons nor <u>his daughter</u> (was) interested in moving.

2.   I was so thirsty that <u>either</u> of the two drinks (was) fine with me.

3.   CORRECT

4.   CORRECT

5.   The recent <u>string</u> of burglaries, in addition to poor building maintenance, (has) inspired the outspoken woman to call a tenants meeting.

6.   There (are), according to my doctor, many <u>courses</u> of treatment available to me.

7.   <u>The sun shining on the flowerbeds</u> (makes) a beautiful sight.

8.   CORRECT

9.   Just around the corner (are) <u>a bakery and a supermarket</u>.

10.   CORRECT

11.   CORRECT

12.   Tired of practicing, <u>the orchestra</u> (decides) to walk out on *its* astonished conductor.

13.   <u>The young bride</u>, as well as her husband, (was) amazed by the generosity of the wedding guests.

14.   Neither she nor <u>her parents</u> (understand) the challenging math problem.

15.   CORRECT

Sentence Correction

Now that you have completed your study of SUBJECT-VERB AGREEMENT, it is time to test your skills on problems that have actually appeared on real GMAT exams over the past several years.

The problem set that follows is composed of past GMAT problems from two books published by GMAC (Graduate Management Admission Council):

The Official Guide for GMAT Review, 11th edition (pages 39-43 & 638-660)
The Official Guide for GMAT Verbal Review (pages 234-253)

The problems in the set below are primarily focused on SUBJECT-VERB AGREEMENT issues. For each of these problems, identify the subjects and verbs and decide whether each is singular or plural. Eliminate answer choices in which the subject and verb do not agree. If word order makes it difficult to evaluate the subject-verb agreement, remember to flip it!

<u>Note</u>: Problem numbers preceded by "D" refer to questions in the Diagnostic Test chapter of *The Official Guide for GMAT Review, 11th edition* (pages 39-43).

Subject-Verb Agreement

11th edition: D41, D43, 1, 3, 21, 34, 41, 42, 52, 61, 70, 90, 116, 131, 138
Verbal Review: 8, 16, 24, 34, 35, 44, 59, 77, 104

Chapter 3
of
SENTENCE CORRECTION

VERB TENSE, MOOD, & VOICE

In This Chapter . . .

VERB TENSE, MOOD, & VOICE

In addition to subject-verb agreement, verbs have three aspects that are tested on the GMAT: tense, mood, and voice.

Verb tense indicates when an action takes place. In sentences with one action, verb tense is relatively easy. Knowing this, the GMAT attempts to make sentences difficult by incorporating more than one action.

There are two moods that are tested on the GMAT: indicative and subjunctive. Verbs in the indicative mood deal with real events. Verbs in the subjunctive mood deal with events that are not necessarily true.

Finally, there are two voices that are tested on the GMAT: active voice and passive voice. In the active voice, the subject of the sentence performs the action. In the passive voice, the subject of the sentence has an action performed on it by someone or something else.

> A split infinitive is
> almost always
> incorrect.

Infinitives

When a verb takes the form **to** + the verb, it is called the infinitive form. This is considered the most basic form of the verb, or the building block of all other tenses. To form other tenses of the verb, you simply modify the infinitive form.

One additional note about the infinitive form: avoid sentences that insert a word (or words) between **to** and the verb. This error is called a split infinitive and, although it is rarely tested on the GMAT, you should know that it is almost always incorrect.

> Incorrect: **I need you TO quickly RUN out to the store.**
> Correct: **I need you TO RUN quickly out to the store.**

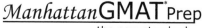

The Simple Tenses

The basic tenses are:

PRESENT (or present progressive)
Sandy plays with her friends (or She is playing with her friends).

PAST (or past progressive)
Sandy played with her friends (or She was playing with her friends).

FUTURE (or future progressive)
Sandy will play with her friends (or She will be playing with her friends).

The progressive tense indicates an ongoing action—in the past, present, or future.

In general, try to use the simple tenses (present, past, and future) instead of the progressive tenses. However, if the meaning of the sentence emphasizes the ongoing nature of an action, you can use the progressive tense. For example:

She was playing with her friends when the babysitter arrived.

Keep It Simple

Sentences with more than one action do not necessarily require more than one verb tense. In fact, unless the actions do not take place at the same time, you should keep all verb tenses in a given sentence the same. For example:

She WALKED to school in the morning and RAN home in the afternoon.
She WALKS to school in the morning and RUNS home in the afternoon.
She WILL WALK to school in the morning and RUN home in the afternoon.

In the first sentence, both verbs are in the past tense. In the second sentence, both verbs are in the present tense. In the third sentence, both verbs are in the future tense. (Note that **run** is understood as **will run**.) There is no reason to change tenses within any of these sentences, so the verb tenses are kept the same.

The Perfect Tenses: An Introduction

Some sentences with more than one action do require you to switch verb tenses within a sentence. Sometimes this involves a simple and logical switch between the simple tenses. For example:

He IS thin now because he SPENT the last six months on an intensive diet.

Here, the first verb is in the present tense (**is**), while the second verb is in the past tense (**spent**). This is a logical switch given the content of the sentence.

Sometimes, however, actions in a sentence involve more complex time sequences. These actions can be expressed using the PERFECT tenses: Present Perfect & Past Perfect. You must understand these to do well on the GMAT.

Present Perfect: Still Going . . .

THE ACTION

A moment in the past   **The present moment**

Use the present perfect tense for an action that began in the past and continues into the present.

If an event started in the past but continues into (or remains true in) the present, you must use the present perfect tense. The present perfect tense is formed as follows:

Present Perfect = HAVE/HAS + Past Participle

The past participle of a regular verb (to walk, to dance, and to jump) is simply the verb with an **-ed** ending, such as **walked**, **danced**, and **jumped**. Irregular verbs (to go, to throw, and to be) have unique past participles, such as **gone**, **thrown**, and **been**.

Here are some examples of actions in the present perfect tense:

We HAVE LIVED in a little hut for three days.
Our country HAS ENFORCED strict immigration laws for thirty years.
They HAVE KNOWN each other for the longest time.

Each example involves an action that began in the past and continues into the present. We lived in a little hut for three days and still live there today. Our country enforced strict immigration laws in the past and still enforces them today. They knew each other in the past and still know each other today. Therefore, each sentence employs the present perfect tense. The first two examples involve regular verbs (that have regular past participles−**lived**, **enforced**), while the third example involves an irregular verb (with an irregular past participle−**known**).

Past Perfect: The Earlier Action

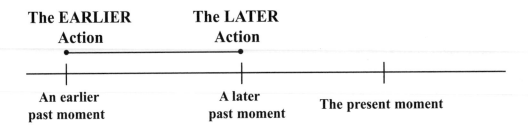

The EARLIER Action

The LATER Action

An earlier
past moment

A later
past moment

The present moment

When forming the past perfect tense, it does not matter which verb comes first in the sentence, only which verb comes first in time.

If more than one action in a sentence occurred at different times in the past, you use the past perfect tense for the earlier action and the simple past for the later action in order to resolve any ambiguity about the sequence. The past perfect tense is formed as follows:

> **Past Perfect = HAD + Past Participle**

The formation of past participles is described on the next page. Here are some examples of sentences that employ the past perfect tense.

> **The film HAD STARTED by the time we ARRIVED at the theater.**
> **The teacher THOUGHT that Jimmy HAD CHEATED on the exam.**

The earlier past action (**had started, had cheated**) is in the past perfect tense, while the later past action is in the simple past tense (**arrived, thought**).

Exceptions to the rule: (1) Verbs that have the same grammatical subject. For instance, **I went to the store and bought milk.** **Went** happened before **bought**, but there's no need to use the past perfect, because the sequence is clear.
(2) Clauses linked by **before** or **after**. These conjunctions indicate the time sequence very clearly, so you do not generally need to use the past perfect tense.

Note that the past perfect tense is the most important and most commonly used of the perfect tenses on the GMAT.

Perfect Tenses: Only When Necessary

Do not use the perfect tenses when the simple tenses will do. Remember that the GMAT prefers simplicity! In the following example, the past perfect (**had believed**) is unnecessary because the sentence involves only one action in the past tense.

> Incorrect: **I think that ancient peoples HAD BELIEVED in many gods.**
> Correct: **I think that ancient peoples BELIEVED in many gods.**

You should only use the perfect tenses when you can justify them with the rules described in this section. If an action began in the past and continues into the present, use the present perfect tense. If an action precedes an earlier past action, use the past perfect tense. Otherwise, stick to the simple tenses.

Past Participles of Irregular Verbs

As you have seen, the perfect tenses are formed by using past participles. Recall that the past participle of a regular verb (such as to walk, to dance, and to jump) is simply the verb with an **-ed** ending, such as **walked**, **danced**, and **jumped**. For irregular verbs, however, there is no hard and fast rule; you must memorize the particular verb formations. The following chart shows some of the most common irregular verbs and their unique forms—both the simple past form and the past participle form:

Verb	Simple Past	Past Participle
BEGIN	She **began** to run.	She has **begun** to run.
BROUGHT	They **brought** their son home.	They have **brought** their son home.
DO	He **did** his work.	He has **done** his work.
DRINK	She **drank** the soda.	She has **drunk** all the soda.
FORGET	She **forgot** her wallet.	She has **forgotten** her wallet.
GET	She **got** her things.	She has **gotten** her things.
GO	He **went** to the store.	He has **gone** to the store.
HANG (object)	She **hung** the picture.	She has **hung** the picture.
HANG (person)	They **hanged** the outlaw.	They have **hanged** the outlaw.
LAY (to put)	He **laid** the plate on the table.	He has **laid** the plate on the table.
LIE (to tell an untruth)	She **lied** about her past.	She has **lied** about her past.
LIE (to recline)	She **lay** on the bed.	He has **lain** on the bed.
RISE	She **rose** for breakfast.	She has **risen** for breakfast.
SWIM	He **swam** in the ocean.	He has **swum** in the ocean.
THROW	She **threw** the ball.	She has **thrown** the ball.

Memorize the irregular simple past and past participle forms of these verbs.

The Verb "To Have"

You may have noticed that in order to form the perfect tenses, all verbs use forms of the helping verb **to have**. What happens if you want to put the verb **to have** itself in the perfect tense? Follow the same formation as any other verb.

> **He HAS HAD many affairs.**
> **His wife divorced him because he HAD HAD an affair.**

In the first example, the verb to have is in the present perfect tense (HAVE/HAS + PAST PARTICIPLE). **Has** signals the present perfect tense while **had** is the past participle of the verb **to have**. In the second example, the verb **to have** is in the past perfect tense (HAD + PAST PARTICIPLE). The first **had** signals the past perfect tense while the second **had** is the past participle of the verb **to have**.

Although they may look strange, **have/has had**, and **had had** are correct verb constructions.

IF . . . THEN Tense Constructions

Sentences that use the word IF to describe hypothetical conditions require a conditional verb construction. These sentences have two parts: the IF clause & the THEN clause.

> **If you study diligently, (then) you will score highly.** OR
> **You will score highly if you study diligently.**

Note that the actual word THEN is frequently omitted. Note also that the IF clause does not have to appear first in the sentence.

IF CLAUSE	THEN CLAUSE
PRESENT	**WILL + BASE VERB**
If she **wins** the lottery,	she **will give** half the money to charity.
If you **study**,	you **will score** highly.
PAST	**WOULD/COULD + BASE VERB**
If she **won** the lottery,	she **would give** half the money to charity.
If you **studied**,	you **would score** highly.
PAST PERFECT	**WOULD/COULD + HAVE + PAST PARTICIPLE**
If she **had won** the lottery,	she **would have given** half the money to charity.
If you **had studied**,	you **would have scored** highly.

> Use the simple past, present, and future tenses unless you have a good reason not to.

When analyzing an IF. . .THEN sentence, perform the following steps:

1) Find the IF clause and label it.
2) Analyze the verb construction in the IF clause. Note that there are only 3 options (as shown in the chart above). Note also that the conditional words **would** and **could** NEVER appear in the IF clause.
3) Find the THEN clause and label it.
4) Analyze the verb construction in the THEN clause. Make sure that the verb construction follows appropriately from the IF clause.

"If" or "Whether"

Note that the word IF does not always signal a conditional sentence.

> **I don't know IF I will go to the dance.**

The IF clause here is not followed by a THEN clause, so this is not a conditional sentence. In this sentence, the word **if** carries the meaning of whether. In such cases, the GMAT prefers that you use the word **whether** instead of **if**.

> **Incorrect: I don't know IF I will go to the dance.**
> **Correct: I don't know WHETHER I will go to the dance.**

The Subjunctive Mood

In English, we do not often use the subjunctive. Most sentences are written in the indicative mood, used to express facts, or the imperative mood, used to express commands. You can expect to see the subjunctive mood in two types of sentences:

(1) IF clauses, when the IF clause expresses a condition contrary to reality.
(2) Hopes, proposals, desires, and requests formed with the word **that**.

If I WERE a Rich Man. . .

The subjunctive case is used to express a degree of uncertainty or unreality. The IF clauses in both of the sentences below express a condition that is untrue. In the first sentence, the speaker actually is NOT rich. In the second sentence, the man in question actually is NOT tall.

> Incorrect: **If I WAS rich, I would donate money to rebuild my old school.**
> Correct: **If I WERE rich, I would donate money to rebuild my old school.**

> Incorrect: **If he WAS tall, he would be able to play basketball better.**
> Correct: **If he WERE tall, he would be able to play basketball better.**

In this use of the subjunctive, the verb **to be** always appears as the word **were**, regardless of the subject. It never appears as the word **was**.

Uncertainty: Hopes, proposals, desires, and requests

The subjunctive is also used to express the desire of one person or body for another person or body to do something. There is a degree of uncertainty as to whether or not the second person or body will actually do what is asked.

> **It is urgent that she SIGN the permission slip.**
> **I respectfully ask that he BE allowed to continue.**
> **My advice is that he simply LOVE her for who she is.**

Note that this use of the subjunctive is formed with the word **that** + **the infinitive form** of the verb (without the word **to**).

This use of the subjunctive follows words and phrases such as advice, advisable, ask, arrange, better, demand, desire, desirable, direct, directive, essential, fitting, imperative, important, insist, instruct, instructions, intend, intentions, necessary, order, pray, prefer, preferable, plead, propose, recommend, request, require, suggest, suggestion, urge, urgent, and vital.

> Incorrect: **The parolee knew it was imperative that he FOUND a job quickly.**
> Correct: **The parolee knew it was imperative that he FIND a job quickly.**

If he was is always wrong on the GMAT.

Active vs. Passive Voice

English verbs are written in either active or passive voice. In the active voice, the subject of the sentence performs the action. In the passive voice, the subject of the sentence has an action performed on it by someone or something else.

The passive voice is formed with a form of **to be**, followed by a participle. The person or people performing the action in the sentence almost always follow the verb.

Although the passive voice is not grammatically incorrect, it often makes sentences longer and more confusing. Also, it often makes it difficult to ascertain who performed the action in the sentence. Since the authors of the GMAT always prefer brevity and simplicity whenever possible, you should usually avoid answer choices written in the passive voice when the passive voice contributes to unnecessary wordiness or confusion.

Passive voice often makes a sentence unnecessarily wordy and awkward.

> Passive: **The pizza WAS EATEN by the hungry students.**
> Active: **The hungry students ate the pizza.**

> Passive: **It HAS BEEN DECIDED by Jason that he will not attend college.**
> Active: **Jason has decided not to attend college.**

You will notice that the corrected sentences are clearer and simpler.

Only transitive verbs (verbs that take direct objects) can be written in the passive voice. Verbs that do not take objects should never be written in the passive voice.

> Incorrect: **The aliens WERE ARRIVED on Neptune in the 20th century.**
> Correct: **The aliens ARRIVED on Neptune in the 20th century.**

> Incorrect: **After they advertised, sales WERE INCREASED by 25%.**
> Correct: **After they advertised, sales INCREASED by 25%.**

Is Passive Voice Ever the Correct Answer?

Passive voice is sometimes, though not frequently, used in a correct answer choice on the GMAT. Consider the following example:

In this operation, new blood vessels are inserted to bypass blocked vessels.

This sentence includes the passive voice verb formation **are inserted**; however, it is not incorrect. The sentence is neither confusing nor wordy. In this sentence, the person performing the action, the unmentioned surgeon, is not important. The focus of the sentence is on the blood vessels being inserted in the operation, rather than on the person inserting them. The passive voice is actually ideal here, as the writer intends to de-emphasize the surgeon and emphasize the action performed on the blood vessels.

The passive voice is also required when the non-underlined portion of the sentence contains the person or agent performing the action preceded by the word **by**. For example, consider the sentence below:

The shuttle launch <u>seen around the world</u> by people of all ages, all races, and all religions.

This sentence is missing a verb, and it is therefore a fragment. Because the **people** who are seeing the launch are at the end of the sentence, preceded by the word **by**, we must use the passive voice to complete this sentence:

The shuttle launch WAS seen around the world by people of all ages, all races, and all religions.

In general, you should avoid passive voice on the GMAT. However, this form may appear in a correct answer choice —especially in science, medical, and technical writing styles.

Problem Set

In each of the following 15 sentences, circle the verbs or verb constructions. Locate all verb-related errors and rewrite each sentence correcting the mistakes. If the sentence is correct as it is, mark it with the word CORRECT.

1. I propose that Amy apologizes to Mark, and we forget this ever happened.

2. We are walking all over the countryside since last weekend.

3. Dylan's work was done quickly by him.

4. Alexandra never insists that Michael calls her after a date, but he does anyway.

5. We thought that Joe didn't go to the museum with the rest of the class.

6. She had already gotten up and was brushing her teeth when the phone rang.

7. Fifty buckets of water were placed on the truck.

8. The attorney proposed that the session was adjourned until the following day.

9. They never met an Australian before they met Crocodile Dundee.

10. Because Helen had homework to do, the television was turned off by her mother.

11. We could start the meeting if Sam was here.

12. All physicians should have been informed of the new regulations by an OSHA representative.

13. If she had had more money, she will have bought herself a new dress.

14. He often asks that Hsiao-Ling bring a tape recorder to the interview sessions.

15. If I wait around any longer, I will be losing my patience.

The following answer key corrects only errors in verb constructions. You may have identified additional verbs or verb constructions that were already correct.

1.   I propose that Amy apologize to Mark, and we forget this ever happened. (*subjunctive*)

2.   We have been walking all over the countryside since last weekend. (*present perfect*)

3.   Dylan did his work quickly. (*active voice*)

4.   Alexandra never insists that Michael call her after a date, but he does anyway. (*subjunctive*)

5.   We thought that Joe hadn't gone to the museum with the rest of the class. (*past perfect*)

6.   CORRECT

7.   CORRECT

8.   The attorney proposed that the session be adjourned until the following day. (*subjunctive*)

9.   They had never met an Australian before they met Crocodile Dundee. (*past perfect*)

10.   Because Helen had homework to do, her mother turned off the television. (*active voice*)

11.   We could start the meeting if Sam were here. (*subjunctive*)

12.   CORRECT

13.   If she had had more money, she would have bought herself a new dress. (*if . . . then*)

14.   CORRECT

15.   If I wait around any longer, I will lose my patience. (*if . . . then*)

Sentence Correction

Now that you have completed your study of VERB TENSE, MOOD, & VOICE, it is time to test your skills on problems that have actually appeared on real GMAT exams over the past several years.

The problem set that follows is composed of past GMAT problems from two books published by GMAC (Graduate Management Admission Council):

The Official Guide for GMAT Review, 11th edition (pages 39-43 & 638-660)
The Official Guide for GMAT Verbal Review (pages 234-253)

The problems in the set below are primarily focused on VERB TENSE, MOOD, & VOICE issues. For each of these problems, identify all verb constructions. For each verb, identify the tense, and (if appropriate) the mood and voice. Eliminate answer choices that contain errors in verb tense, mood, or voice.

<u>Note</u>: Problem numbers preceded by "D" refer to questions in the Diagnostic Test chapter of *The Official Guide for GMAT Review, 11th edition* (pages 39-43).

Verb Tense, Mood, & Voice
> *11th edition:* D39, 15, 28, 57, 58, 59, 62, 63, 74, 75, 76, 81, 83, 94, 108, 126, 137
> *Verbal Review:* 3, 13, 21, 28, 30, 37, 40, 65, 83, 86, 95, 103

Chapter 4
of
SENTENCE CORRECTION

PRONOUNS

In This Chapter . . .

- Pronoun Reference
- Pronoun Agreement
- Pronoun Case
- Possessive Poison
- The Deadly Four: It, Its, They, Their

PRONOUNS

A pronoun is a word that takes the place of a noun. For example, in the sentence below, the pronouns **he** and **it** replace the nouns **Sam** and **ball**.

Sam played with the ball. HE played with IT.

GMAT pronoun errors are so frequent that every time you see a pronoun in a GMAT sentence, you should immediately stop to see if it is being used correctly. Although pronoun errors are prevalent, the good news is that there are only 3 types of pronoun mistakes that the GMAT tests: Pronoun Reference, Pronoun Agreement, and Pronoun Case.

Pronoun Reference

The first question you must ask yourself when you see a pronoun is this: To which noun (or other pronoun) does this pronoun refer? Or, which noun is the pronoun replacing?

> Every pronoun must refer to only one antecedent.

Eva exercised daily so that SHE would stay in good shape.

Here the pronoun **she** clearly refers to **Eva**. The noun to which the pronoun refers is the antecedent, or the referent. Thus, **Eva** is the antecedent of the pronoun **she**.

Every pronoun on the GMAT must clearly refer to one and only one antecedent. There may be no ambiguity as to what the antecedent is. Sentences in which there are two or more possible antecedents for a given pronoun should be rewritten so that there is only one possible pronoun referent.

Eva exercised daily with Jasmine so that SHE would stay in good shape.

In this example, the pronoun **she** does not have one clear antecedent. **She** seems to be referring to **Jasmine** (as Jasmine is the closest noun), but it also could be referring to **Eva**. We can correct this ambiguity by rewriting the sentence as follows:

Eva hoped to stay in good shape, so SHE exercised daily with Jasmine.

Sometimes you will find a GMAT sentence in which a pronoun has no true antecedent at all, although an antecedent seems to be implied. Implication is not enough; there must be a stated antecedent for every GMAT pronoun. For example:

Friendship was something James truly valued, so he disliked it when THEY talked about him behind his back.

Here the pronouns **he**, **him**, and **his** clearly refer to James. However, the pronoun **they** has no antecedent at all. One might think that **they** refers to James's friends, but the word **friends** is never mentioned in the sentence; only the word **friendship** is. Therefore, the preceding sentence is incorrect.

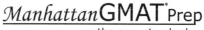

Manhattan GMAT* Prep
the new standard

Pronoun Agreement

After finding the antecedent, ask yourself a second question: Does the pronoun agree with the antecedent in number? If the antecedent is singular, the pronoun that refers to it must be singular. If the antecedent is plural, the pronoun that refers to it must be plural.

> **Police work is very important as THEY help to enforce the laws of the state.**

Here, the pronoun **they** is plural. However, its logical antecedent **police work** is singular. In order to correct this error, either change the pronoun or change the antecedent:

> **Policemen are very important as THEY help to enforce the laws of the state.**
> **Police work is very important as IT is the backbone of law enforcement.**

There are 3 pronoun cases: subject, object, and possessive.

Pronoun Case

The third and final question you must ask yourself when analyzing a GMAT pronoun is the following: Is the pronoun in the proper case, given its use in the sentence? This question is most applicable to personal pronouns and the pronoun **who**.

SUBJECT pronouns	OBJECT pronouns	POSSESSIVE pronouns
I	me	my, mine
you	you	your, yours
he	him	his
she	her	her, hers
it	it	its (not it's!)
we	us	our, ours
they	them	their, theirs
who	whom	whose

> Incorrect: **Janice and ME went on a picnic together.**
> Correct: **Janice and I went on a picnic together.**

The pronoun is part of the subject of the sentence, so the correct form is **I**, not **me**.

> Incorrect: **The picnic was attended by Janice and I.**
> Correct: **The picnic was attended by Janice and ME.**

Picnic is the subject of the sentence, while the pronoun is part of the object of the sentence; thus the correct form is **me**, not **I**.

> Incorrect: **WHO are you going to marry?**
> Correct: **WHOM are you going to marry?**

You is the subject of this sentence, while the pronoun is the object; thus the correct form is **whom**, not **who**.

Possessive Poison

Possessive nouns are particularly dangerous on the GMAT. Consider the following:

Jose's room is so messy that HIS mother calls HIM a pig.

The possessive noun in this sentence is **Jose's**. Possessive pronouns can refer back to possessive nouns. Thus the possessive pronoun **his** refers back to **Jose's**. However, subject and object pronouns may NOT refer back to possessive nouns. Therefore, the object pronoun **him** is used incorrectly because it may not refer back to **Jose's**. Subject and object pronouns may only refer back to subject and object nouns. **Him** would only be accurate if it referred back to the word **Jose**.

Even though it seems obvious that **him** refers to **Jose**, the sentence must be changed in order for it to be grammatically correct on the GMAT. We can fix the sentence by keeping **his** and eliminating **him**.

Jose's room is so messy that his mother calls Jose a pig.

Its is a possessive pronoun. **It's** is a contraction, meaning *it is*.

The Deadly Four: It, Its, They, Their

The most common pronoun mistakes involve third person personal pronouns — the singular **it** and its possessive **its**, and the plural **they** and its possessive **their**. Whenever you see one of these four pronouns, you should stop and make sure that it agrees in number with its antecedent.

Their is the possessive form of the plural pronoun **they**, so **their** can only refer to a plural subject. Unfortunately, in everyday speech **their** is used incorrectly as the possessive of singular subjects.

> Incorrect: **When the person calls, take down THEIR information.**
> Correct: **When the person calls, take down HIS information. OR**
> Correct: **When the people call, take down THEIR information.**

The antecedent **person** is singular, so it requires the singular pronoun **his** or **her**, not the plural pronoun **their**. If one changes the antecedent to the plural **people**, one can use the plural pronoun **their**.

> Incorrect: **Everyone here will need THEIR own pencil.**
> Correct: **Everyone here will need HIS own pencil.**

The antecedent **everyone** is singular (see Subject-Verb Agreement). Therefore, it requires the singular pronoun **his**, not the plural pronoun **their**.

Problem Set

In each of the following 15 sentences, underline all important pronouns. Then, for each pronoun, perform the 3-question test:

1) <u>What is the antecedent of the pronoun?</u> If you can locate it, underline it. If the antecedent is unclear or not there at all, rewrite the sentence correcting the error.

2) <u>Do the pronoun and antecedent agree in number?</u> If they do, mark with a check. If they do not, rewrite the sentence correcting the error.

3) <u>Is the pronoun in the proper case?</u> If it is, mark with a check. If it is not, rewrite the sentence correcting the error.

1. Who are you going to take to the movies?

2. Kathy's suitcase was so stuffed that she decided to pack another one.

3. The students' work improved over the course of the semester, and they should be commended for it.

4. The players' helmets need to be repainted so that they will be ready to be used at practice on Sunday.

5. I don't understand why me and Bob always have to take out the garbage.

6. Some people believe that the benefits of a healthy diet outweigh that of regular exercise.

7. We finally chose the coffee table towards the back of the store, which we thought would complement our living room furniture.

8. At the end of the day, the chaperones took the fourth graders back to school, who were exhausted from running after the children.

9. Everyone here needs their own copy of the textbook in order to take this class.

10. Samantha's face looked blurry in the photo, but I could tell she wasn't smiling.

11. We finally returned all the books to the library, which we left at the front desk.

12. Jim may not be elected CEO by the board because he does not meet their standards.

13. Meg left all her class notes at school because she decided that she could do her homework without it.

14. The person who cheated on the test should raise their hand.

15. Only pack the clothes that you are planning to wear.

1.   *Whom* are you going to take to the movies?

2.   Kathy's suitcase was so stuffed that *Kathy* decided to pack another one.

3.   The students' work improved over the course of the semester, and *the students* should be commended for it.

4.   CORRECT

5.   I don't understand why Bob and *I* always have to take out the garbage.

6.   Some people believe that the benefits of a healthy diet outweigh *those* of regular exercise.

7.   We finally chose the coffee table towards the back of the store, *because* we thought *it* would complement our living room furniture.

8.   At the end of the day, the chaperones, *who were exhausted from running after the children,* took the fourth graders back to school.

9.   Everyone here needs *his or her* own copy of the textbook in order to take this class.

10.   Samantha's face looked blurry in the photo, but I could tell *Samantha* wasn't smiling.

11.   We finally returned all the books, *leaving them at the library's front desk.*

12.   Jim may not be elected CEO by the board because he does not meet *its* standards.

13.   Meg left all her class notes at school because she decided that she could do her homework without *them.*

14.   The person who cheated on the test should raise *his or her* hand.

15.   CORRECT

Sentence Correction

Now that you have completed your study of PRONOUNS, it is time to test your skills on problems that have actually appeared on real GMAT exams over the past several years.

The problem set that follows is composed of past GMAT problems from two books published by GMAC (Graduate Management Admission Council):

The Official Guide for GMAT Review, 11th edition (pages 39-43 & 638-660)
The Official Guide for GMAT Verbal Review (pages 234-253)

The problems in the set below are primarily focused on PRONOUN issues. For each of these problems, identify each pronoun and its antecedent. Eliminate any answer choices that contain errors in pronoun use, including missing or unclear antecedents, agreement errors (in case or number), possessive poison, and incorrect uses of relative pronouns.

Note: Problem numbers preceded by "D" refer to questions in the Diagnostic Test chapter of *The Official Guide for GMAT Review, 11th edition* (pages 39-43).

Pronouns

     11th edition: D42, 5, 25, 32, 43, 89, 127, 130, 133
     Verbal Review: 12, 15, 19, 29, 41, 49, 53, 55, 58, 61, 67, 71, 72, 74, 85, 89, 102

g

Chapter 5
of
SENTENCE CORRECTION

MODIFIERS

In This Chapter . . .

- Adjectives and Adverbs
- Modifying Phrases
- Possessive Poison Yet Again
- Adverbial Modifiers
- Modifiers with Relative Pronouns
- Essential vs. Non-essential Modifiers
- Punctuating Essential and Non-essential Modifiers
- Ensuring Clarity in Modifiers Introduced by "Which"

MODIFIERS

A modifier, or a modifying phrase, describes someone or something in the sentence. Although modifiers can be as simple as a single word—an adjective or an adverb—GMAT sentences will often contain complex modifying phrases and multiple modifiers. It is important to be able to identify all the modifying phrases in a given sentence.

> **Tired out from playing basketball, Charles decided to take a nap.**

The modifying phrase **tired out from playing basketball** is a descriptive group of words that describes **Charles**.

Often, modifying phrases in GMAT sentences are separated from the noun being modified by commas. Be on the lookout for opening modifiers, which appear in the beginning of a sentence. In the example above, **tired out from playing basketball** is an opening modifier, separated from the rest of the sentence by a comma.

Modifiers are usually set off from the rest of the sentence by commas.

Adjectives and Adverbs

An adjective modifies a noun or pronoun. An adverb usually modifies a verb, but it can also describe an adjective, another adverb, a preposition, or a phrase.

> **The SMART man acts QUICKLY.**

Adjective	Adverb
nice	nicely
quick	quickly
slow	slowly
smooth	smoothly

Here the adjective **smart** modifies the noun **man**, while the adverb **quickly** modifies the verb **acts**. Many adverbs are formed by adding **-ly** to the adjective.

Be sure not to use an adjective where an adverb is required:

Incorrect: **My friend Katy is a REAL interesting person.**
Correct: **My friend Katy is a REALLY interesting person.**

The adverb **really**, not the adjective **real**, must be used to modify the adjective **interesting**. Remember that adjectives *only* modify *nouns*, while adverbs modify verbs, adjectives, or other adverbs.

Note also the distinction between the words **good** and **well**. **Good** is an adjective that describes a noun. **Well** can be used either as an adjective that means **healthy**, or as an adverb that means **competently**.

> **Amy is a GOOD person.** (**Good** is an adjective modifying the noun **person**.)
> **Amy is feeling WELL.** (**Well** is an adjective modifying the noun **Amy**.)
> **Amy writes WELL.** (**Well** is an adverb modifying the verb **writes**.)

Modifying Phrases

After finding a modifying phrase, find the noun that is being modified. In some cases, the noun will not be there at all. This is called a dangling modifier. For example:

Using the latest technology, the mechanical problem was identified quickly.

Here, the modifier **using the latest technology** is probably describing a technician who identified the problem. However, a technician never appears in the sentence. Instead, the phrase **using the latest technology** seems to modify **the mechanical problem**. Clearly, the mechanical problem did not use the latest technology. In order to correct this problem, we can insert a noun which the modifier can modify:

Using the latest technology, the engineer identified the problem quickly.

In some cases, the modified noun will be in the sentence but it will not be *directly* next to the modifying phrase. This is called a misplaced modifier. For example:

Upon leaving the register, the cashier handed the customer a receipt.

Here, the modifier **upon leaving the register** seems to modify **the cashier**, although it should modify **the customer**. In order to correct this, we must place the modifying phrase directly next to what it modifies.

Upon leaving the register, the customer received a receipt from the cashier.

A modifying phrase should not be separated from the noun that it modifies.

Kendra is happy, like all her friends, to be on vacation.

The modifying phrase **like all her friends** clearly modifies **Kendra**. However, the sentence should be rewritten so that the modifier touches the noun that it modifies:

Kendra, like all her friends, is happy to be on vacation.
(OR) Like all her friends, Kendra is happy to be on vacation.

Here is another example:

Jim biked along a dirt road to get to his house, which was long and windy and cut through the woods.

In the preceding example, the modifying phrase **which was long and windy and cut through the woods** describes **the dirt road**, not **the house**. Therefore, the sentence can be corrected by moving the modifier so that it is right next to the noun **dirt road**.

In order to get to his house, Jim biked along a dirt road, which was long and windy and cut through the woods.

The modifier should touch the noun that it modifies.

Possessive Poison Yet Again

Just as possessive nouns are often dangerous with regard to pronoun reference, they are also dangerous in sentences with modifiers. Very often, dangling modifiers appear in sentences that have possessive nouns. For example:

> **Unskilled in complex math, Bill's score on the entrance exam was poor.**

Here, the modifier **unskilled in complex math** should describe **Bill**. However, **Bill** never appears in the sentence; only **Bill's score** appears. Clearly, Bill's score is not unskilled in complex math. To correct the sentence, we can replace the possessive **Bill's score** with **Bill**.

> **Unskilled in complex math, Bill did not score well on the entrance exam.**

Adverbial modifiers do not need to touch the words they modify.

Adverbial Modifiers

A modifier and its modified noun should always touch. However, when the word being modified is not a noun, the modifying phrase is called an adverbial phrase and does not need to touch the word being modified. For example,

> **The running back ran towards the end zone, faster and harder than he had ever run before.**

In this sentence, the phrase **faster and harder than he had ever run before** describes *how* the running back *ran*. Thus, the phrase is not modifying **the running back**; instead, it is modifying **ran**. If the modifier answers the question *how?* about a verb, it is an adverbial modifier.

Note that although an adverbial modifier does not need to touch the verb it modifies, it should be placed in the sentence in such a way as to avoid ambiguity regarding which word it is modifying. For example,

> **The group arrived in New Orleans and decided to stay in a fancy hotel a week before Mardi Gras.**

The adverbial modifier **a week before Mardi Gras** describes when the group **arrived** in New Orleans. However, the adverbial modifier is incorrectly placed closer to the verb **decided** than to the verb **arrived**, implying that the group's decision was made **a week before Mardi Gras**. The sentence can be corrected by moving the adverbial modifier closer to the word **arrived**, as shown below.

> **The group arrived in New Orleans a week before Mardi Gras and decided to stay in a fancy hotel.**

Modifiers with Relative Pronouns

Modifying phrases are often introduced by relative pronouns such as:

which, that, where, who, whose, whom

Relative pronouns are helpful when other ways of inserting a modifier are awkward.

> Awkward: **We test-drove a car having engine trouble.**
> Correct: **We test-drove a car THAT had engine trouble.**

> Awkward: **The Yankees, never liking to lose, practice every day.**
> Correct: **The Yankees, WHO never like to lose, practice every day.**

On the GMAT, it is sometimes preferable to insert a modifier using a relative pronoun and a simple verb tense than using just an **-ing** form of a verb. Notice that in the sentences above, the words **having** and **liking** have been replaced with the words **had** and **like**.

 The pronoun **who** introduces phrases that modify a person or a group of people, while the pronoun **which** introduce phrases that modify things. The pronoun **that** can be used to modify either people or things.

Essential vs. Non-essential Modifiers

Which is used to introduce "non-essential" modifiers. These are clauses that provide information about a noun that is *not* necessary for identifying that noun.
That is used to introduce "essential" modifiers. These are clauses that provide information about a noun that *is* necessary for identifying that noun.

This may sound complicated, but look at the following examples:

> Non-essential: To find my house, walk down the left side of the street until you reach the third house, **which** is red.
> Essential: To find my house, walk down the left side of the street until you reach the third house **that** is red.

Do the two sentences above lead you to the same house? Not necessarily. The first sentence (using the non-essential clause **which is red**) always leads you to the THIRD house on the left side of the street. This house happens to be red.

The second sentence (using the essential clause **that is red**) leads you to the third RED house on the left side of the street. This may be the third house on the left side of the street (if the first two are also red), or it may be the eighth house on the left side of the street, or the tenth house, etc.

 A modifier introduced by the word **which** can be removed from the sentence without the sentence losing any essential meaning. On the other hand, a modifier introduced by the word **that** is essential to the meaning of the sentence.

Which is used to introduce non-essential modifiers, **that** is used to introduce essential modifiers, and **who** can introduce either essential or non-essential modifiers.

*Manhattan*GMAT*Prep
the new standard

Punctuating Essential and Non-essential Modifiers

The pronoun **who(m)** is used only for clauses where a person is the subject, but it can be used in either essential or non-essential modifiers.

Non-essential: This is my Uncle John, **who** lives in Toronto.

Essential: This is my Uncle John **who** lives in Toronto.

In the first sentence, the fact that Uncle John lives in Toronto is not essential to his identity (the author likely has only one Uncle John). In the second sentence, however, the fact that Uncle John lives in Toronto is essential to his identity (perhaps the author has another Uncle John in another city).

Notice that the only difference between the two sentences is the use of the comma. In the first sentence, the non-essential clause *is* separated from the subject **Uncle John** by a comma. In the second sentence, the essential clause is *not* separated from the subject **Uncle John** by a comma.

> Commas are used to separate non-essential modifiers from the noun that is modified.

You can see that it is very important to pay attention to whether a modifier should be set off by a comma or not, since this will impact the meaning of the sentence. Non-essential clauses are usually set off from the main clause by commas, whereas essential clauses are not. Consider another example:

The pool is open for the use of guests only in the accompaniment of tenants.

A dog of a sentence! Which of the following is a better replacement?

Only guests who are accompanied by tenants may use the pool.
Only guests, who are accompanied by tenants, may use the pool.

The first sentence identifies a specific subgroup of guests to whom the pool is open: those accompanied by tenants (as opposed to those unaccompanied by tenants).

By contrast, the second sentence indicates (somewhat illogically) that only guests (as opposed to tenants) may use the pool, and that they just happen to be accompanied by tenants.

A problem arises here because the second sentence contains—by mere dint of a pair of commas—an inappropriate non-essential clause where an essential clause is required instead. If an answer choice differs from the original sentence in that it sets a clause apart with commas, you must ask yourself whether the sentence requires an essential or non-essential clause to preserve its logical meaning.

Ensuring Clarity in Modifiers Introduced by "Which"

When used incorrectly, a modifier introduced by the word **which** can change the meaning of a sentence:

> **The police found the murder weapon, which made the prosecutor's job much easier.**

The logical meaning of this sentence is clear: Finding the murder weapon made the prosecutor's job much easier.

However, on the GMAT, when **which** is used as a relative pronoun, it refers to the noun immediately preceding it—not to the action of the entire preceding clause. In this light, the sentence above literally states that it was not the finding of the murder weapon that helped the prosecutor, but rather the murder weapon itself. This is illogical, so the sentence must be rewritten to reflect its logical meaning:

> **The police found the murder weapon, making the prosecutor's job much easier.**

By eliminating **which**, it becomes clear that the modifier **making the prosecutor's job much easier** refers to the finding of the murder weapon, not to the murder weapon itself.

If **which** seems to refer to the action of the preceding clause, you must look among the choices for an alternative that either links **which** properly with a noun antecedent, or that reworks the sentence to avoid the use of **which** entirely.

The relative pronoun **which** *often signals trouble in GMAT sentences, so be on the lookout.*

Problem Set

In each of the following 15 sentences, underline all modifying phrases. Then, identify the noun that is being modified. If there is a modification error, rewrite the sentence correcting the mistake. If the sentence is correct as it is, mark it with the word CORRECT.

1. Upon entering the restaurant, the *maitre d'* handed us a menu.

2. Working diligently and carefully, the faucet was fixed in no time at all.

3. Employing groundbreaking techniques in alternative medicine, the patient's health improved in a few days.

4. David tried a handful of desserts from the table, which ultimately gave him an upset stomach.

5. Like other students in his class, Jim doesn't like to be singled out for making mistakes.

6. Uninterested in the lecture, the orator put most of the audience to sleep.

7. Weary from travel, a dip in the hot tub sounded like a great idea to us.

8. John was thrilled, like the other members of the debate team, to participate in the tournament.

9. The quick-witted hostess pitched a tent over the garden party, a way to protect the guests from the imminent rain.

10. Similar in so many ways, the parents were still able to distinguish between the twins.

11. Based on the recent decline in enrollment, the admissions office decided to reevaluate its recruitment strategies.

12. Unaccustomed to the rigors of college life, James's grades dropped.

13. Mary returned the dress to the store, which was torn at one of the seams.

14. We enjoy meeting people having different interests.

15. Obstinate and surly, the manager's attitude alienated his employees.

1.   <u>Upon entering the restaurant,</u> *we* were handed a menu by the *maitre d'*.

2.   <u>Working diligently and carefully,</u> *she* fixed the faucet in no time at all.

3.   <u>Employing groundbreaking techniques in alternative medicine,</u> *the doctors* saw the patient's health improve in a few days.

4.   David tried a handful of the table's *desserts*, <u>which ultimately gave him an upset stomach.</u>

5.   CORRECT

6.   The orator put most of the *audience*, <u>which was uninterested in the lecture,</u> to sleep.

7.   <u>Weary from travel,</u> *we* thought a dip in the hot tub sounded like a great idea.

8.   *John*, <u>like the other members of the debate team,</u> was thrilled to participate in the tournament.

9.   The quick-witted hostess pitched a *tent* <u>that protected the guests at the garden party from the imminent rain.</u>

10.   <u>Similar in so many ways,</u> the *twins* could still be distinguished by their parents.

11.   <u>Because of the recent decline in enrollment,</u> the admissions office decided to reevaluate its recruitment strategies. (NOTE: Change "Based on" to "Because of." "Based on" modifies the SUBJECT; this modification is incorrect. "Because of" correctly modifies the VERB instead.)

12.   <u>Unaccustomed to the rigors of college life,</u> *James* allowed his grades to drop.

13.   Mary returned the *dress*, <u>which was torn at one of the seams,</u> to the store.

14.   We enjoy meeting *people* <u>who have different interests.</u>

15.   The manager's <u>obstinate and surly</u> *attitude* alienated his employees.

Sentence Correction

Now that you have completed your study of MODIFIERS, it is time to test your skills on problems that have actually appeared on real GMAT exams over the past several years.

The problem set that follows is composed of past GMAT problems from two books published by GMAC (Graduate Management Admission Council):

The Official Guide for GMAT Review, 11th edition (pages 39-43 & 638-660)
The Official Guide for GMAT Verbal Review (pages 234-253)

The problems in the set below are primarily focused on MODIFIER issues. For each of these problems, identify any modifiers and the words that they modify. Eliminate any answer choices that contain modifier errors, including dangling or misplaced modifiers, modifiers that require relative pronouns, and errors in adjective or adverb use.

<u>Note</u>: Problem numbers preceded by "D" refer to questions in the Diagnostic Test chapter of *The Official Guide for GMAT Review, 11th edition* (pages 39-43).

Modifiers

11th edition: D40, D44, D49, 7, 20, 24, 38, 45, 50, 71, 72, 78, 93, 98, 102, 105, 107, 109, 110, 114, 125, 135
Verbal Review: 7, 18, 32, 38, 39, 57, 63, 73, 78, 79, 84, 88, 91, 96, 107, 110, 112

Chapter 6
of
SENTENCE CORRECTION

PARALLELISM

In This Chapter . . .

- Parallel Structures
- Parallelism with Pronouns
- Idioms with Built-In Parallel Structure
- Superficial Parallelism vs. Actual Parallelism
- Watch Out for Verbs of Being

PARALLELISM

The GMAT's favorite grammar topic is parallelism. For a sentence to be grammatically correct on the GMAT, its individual parts must be parallel. Although parallelism does not affect every sentence, it impacts a large percentage of them. Parallelism dictates that comparable sentence parts must be structurally similar. The following example demonstrates a sentence that lacks parallel structure:

> **The employees were upset by their low pay, poor working conditions, and that they did not have many outlets for their creativity.**

Notice that this example has three comparable parts—the three items that upset the employees. The structure of the first two parts is similar; both parts consist of a noun phrase (centered on the nouns **pay** and **conditions**). However, the third part has a different structure altogether; it is a clause consisting of a subject, verb, and object. In order to make the sentence parallel, we must change the third item so that its structure is like that of the first two items (a noun phrase):

> **The employees were upset by their low pay, poor working conditions, and shortage of creative outlets.**

Parallel Structures

There are many different types of parallel structures, from the very simple to the complex. The following chart identifies the most commonly tested of these structures:

Nouns	Trevor collects *stamps*, *coins*, and *cards*.
Adjectives	The wait staff was *prompt*, *friendly*, and *competent*.
Modified Nouns	A positive attitude can lead to both *practical success* and *spiritual fulfillment*.
Verbs	We *worked* all day, *ate* all evening, and *slept* all night.
Verb Infinitives	I decided *to swim* across the river rather than *sail* around the world. (The second *to* is optional.)
Participial Phrases	The rain continued to fall, *providing water* for the thirsty plants but *flooding the streets* as well.
Adverbs	I've noticed that you often howl *angrily* after you cower *fearfully*.
Adverbial Phrases	I've noticed that you often howl *in anger* after you cower *in fear*.

When you are attempting to create parallelism within a GMAT sentence, you should try to use one of the above structures as your model.

When working with parallel infinitives, it is acceptable to leave out the word **to** in all the infinitives after the first.

Parallelism with Pronouns

Often, pronouns—such as **which**, **that**, **those**, **who**, etc.—signal parallel structures. If one item includes a pronoun, it is often appropriate to include the same pronoun in parallel items. For example:

> Incorrect: **I prefer to hire employees WHO work hard to those THAT don't.**
> Correct: **I prefer to hire employees WHO work hard to those WHO don't.**

Pronoun phrases can also help to make sentence parts parallel:

> Incorrect: **Ralph likes a variety of people, including THOSE WHO are popular and WHO are not.**
> Correct: **Ralph likes a variety of people, including THOSE WHO are popular and THOSE WHO are not.**

Make sure the two sides of the sentence are both structurally and logically parallel.

Idioms with Built-In Parallel Structure

Idioms are a topic in and of themselves, which will be treated later on. However, certain idioms are directly related to parallelism in that their structure demands it. The chart shown below lists some idiomatic structures that require parallelism:

In all of these examples, X must be parallel to Y in both structure and meaning. For example:

> Incorrect: **I definitely prefer eating ice cream to hot dogs in the summertime.**
>
> Correct: **In the summertime, I definitely prefer eating ice cream to eating hot dogs.**

Notice that the correct version of this sentence maintains parallel structure within the idiom: **eating ice cream** is parallel to **eating hot dogs**. The phrase **in the summertime** has been moved to the front, so that

Idioms with Parallel Structures
More X than Y
The more X the greater Y
No less was X than was Y
As X to Y
Not only X but also Y
Not X but rather Y
X instead of Y
The same to X as to Y
Range from X to Y
Both X and Y
Either X or Y
Neither X nor Y
Mistake X for Y
Prefer X to Y
X regarded as Y
To think of X as Y
Believe X to be Y

Superficial Parallelism vs. Actual Parallelism

To preserve parallel structure, it is important to pay attention to which grammatical structures—verb phrases, noun phrases, prepositional phrases, adverbial phrases, etc.— are logically parallel before assuming that they must be structurally parallel. For example:

> **Ken traveled around the world, visiting historic sites, eating native foods, and learning about new cultures.**

In the sentence above, the verb phrases **visiting historic sites**, **eating native foods**, and **learning about new cultures** are parallel. The main clause, **traveled around the world**, is not parallel to these verb phrases. This is NOT incorrect. **Traveled** is the main verb, and the other verb phrases provide additional information about what Ken did while traveling. It would distort the meaning of the sentence to change it as follows:

> **Ken traveled around the world, visited historic sites, ate native foods, and learned about new cultures.**

This version gives all the activities equal emphasis, instead of making the last three activities subordinate to the main activity of traveling around the world.

Do not become a victim of superficial parallelism by assuming that ALL verbs in a sentence must be parallel. Only the structures that are logically parallel must be structurally parallel.

Watch Out for Verbs of Being

A more subtle example of parallelism involves verbs of being. Usually, we think of verbs as action words (walk, dance, and jump), but a second class of verbs is termed verbs of being. Instead of expressing what a subject does, these verbs express what a subject is, or the condition a subject is in. The most common verb of being is the verb **to be**, but there are other being verbs as well. Below are two lists. The first contains all the forms of the verb **to be,** while the second contains other common verbs of being:

To Be	Other Verbs of Being or Condition	
is	appear	seem
am	become	smell
are	feel	sound
was	grow	stay
were	look	taste
been	remain	turn
being		

*Manhattan*GMAT Prep
the new standard

When you see a form of the verb **to be** (or any other verb of being), be sure that the two sides of the verb are parallel.

For example:

> **The flower bouquet WAS the husband's giving of love to his wife.**

The two sides of the being verb **was** are **flower bouquet** and **husband's giving of love**. These two sides are not structurally parallel. In order to achieve parallelism, we can rewrite the sentence replacing **giving** with the noun **gift**, so that the two sides of the being verb are structurally similar.

> **The flower bouquet WAS the husband's loving gift to his wife.**

Do not be a victim of superficial parallelism!

In addition to being structurally parallel, you must also ensure that the two sides of the being verb are parallel in meaning. For example:

> **The attitudes of that politician always SEEM TO BE attacking the poor.**

The two sides of the being verb phrase **seem to be** are **attitudes** and **attacking the poor**. However, **attitudes** do not **attack**, so the two sides of the sentence are not parallel in that they do not match up in meaning. In order to achieve parallel meaning, we can rewrite the sentence so that the **politician** himself is doing the **attacking**.

> **Because of his intolerant attitude, that politician always SEEMS TO BE attacking the poor.**

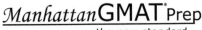

Problem Set

In each of the following 15 sentences, underline each individual sentence part. Then, rewrite each sentence ensuring structural and logical parallelism among the sentence parts.

1. The connection between regular exercise and performing well in school continues to elude us.

2. Although we were sitting in the bleachers, the baseball game was as exciting to us as the people sitting behind home plate.

3. Many teachers have chosen to seek employment in the suburbs rather than facing low salaries in the city.

4. If he is not given ample recovery time after the operation, he is liable to be disoriented and may not perform routine tasks well.

5. Many agree that how you dress for a job interview and even the way you position yourself in your seat leave a lasting impression on your interviewer.

6. A good night's sleep not only gives your body a chance to rest, but energizing you for the following day.

7. The joint business venture will increase employee satisfaction and start improving the relations between upper management and staff.

8. The works displayed in the photography exhibit were contributed by numerous artists, from those who already had mass appeal to who had never had much exposure.

9. We were dismayed to learn that most of our neighbors were unfriendly, disagreeable, and were uninteresting to make new friends.

10. The students did poorly on the test more because they hadn't studied than not understanding the material.

11. The snow covered the train tracks by more than a foot, prompted the transit authority to shut down service temporarily, and causing discontent among commuters who were left stranded for hours.

12. The experiences we had when children still influence our behavior in adulthood.

13. The band chosen for the annual spring concert appealed to the student body and the administration as well.

14. The new toy was the young mother's trying to appease her sobbing child.

15. We decided to walk to the cinema rather than taking the bus.

1. The connection between <u>exercising regularly</u> and <u>performing well in school</u> continues to elude us.

2. Although we were sitting in the bleachers, the baseball game was as exciting <u>to us</u> as <u>to the people sitting behind home plate</u>.

3. Many teachers have chosen to <u>seek employment</u> in the suburbs rather than <u>face low salaries</u> in the city.

4. If he is not given ample recovery time after the operation, he <u>may be disoriented</u> and <u>may not perform routine tasks well</u>.

5. Many agree that <u>how you dress</u> for a job interview and even <u>how you position yourself</u> in your seat leave a lasting impression on your interviewer.

6. A good night's sleep <u>not only gives</u> your body a chance to rest, <u>but also energizes</u> you for the following day.

7. The joint business venture will <u>increase employee satisfaction</u> and <u>improve relations</u> between upper management and staff.

8. The works displayed in the photography exhibit were contributed by numerous artists, from <u>those who already had mass appeal</u> to <u>those who had never had much exposure</u>.

9. We were dismayed to learn that most of our neighbors were <u>unfriendly</u>, <u>disagreeable</u>, and <u>uninterested</u> in making new friends.

10. The students did poorly on the test more <u>because they hadn't studied</u> than <u>because they didn't understand</u> the material.

11. The snow covered the train tracks by more than a foot, <u>prompting</u> the transit authority to shut down service temporarily and <u>causing</u> discontent among commuters who were left stranded for hours.

12. The experiences we had <u>in childhood</u> still influence our behavior <u>in adulthood</u>.

13. The band chosen for the annual spring concert appealed to both <u>the student body</u> and <u>the administration</u>.

14. The new <u>toy</u> was the young mother's <u>attempt</u> to appease her sobbing child.

15. We decided to <u>walk</u> to the cinema rather than <u>take</u> the bus.

Sentence Correction

Now that you have completed your study of PARALLELISM, it is time to test your skills on problems that have actually appeared on real GMAT exams over the past several years.

The problem set that follows is composed of past GMAT problems from two books published by GMAC (Graduate Management Admission Council):

The Official Guide for GMAT Review, 11ᵗʰ edition (pages 39-43 & 638-660)
The Official Guide for GMAT Verbal Review (pages 234-253)

The problems in the set below are primarily focused on PARALLELISM issues. For each of these problems, identify grammatical structures that require parallelism, including lists, idioms, and verbs of being. Be sure to keep all appropriate parts of speech parallel, including pronouns when applicable. Do not fall victim to superficial parallelism!

Note: Problem numbers preceded by "D" refer to questions in the Diagnostic Test chapter of *The Official Guide for GMAT Review, 11ᵗʰ edition* (pages 39-43).

Parallelism

> *11ᵗʰ edition:* D36, D38, D46, D48, D50, 9, 11, 17, 18, 19, 22, 35, 39, 46, 47, 48, 49, 54, 56, 60, 64, 65, 84, 86, 88, 91, 106, 112, 113, 115, 117, 119, 129, 132, 134, 136
> *Verbal Review:* 1, 4, 6, 11, 25, 27, 47, 51, 52, 56, 62, 64, 70, 81, 82, 97, 99, 100

Chapter 7
of
SENTENCE CORRECTION

COMPARISONS

In This Chapter . . .

- "Like" vs. "As"
- Keeping Comparisons Parallel
- Comparative and Superlative Forms

COMPARISONS

Comparisons are a special form of parallelism that deserve special attention. Comparisons always compare at least two things. Although they may seem simple, comparisons within a sentence are often complex and subtle.

In attacking GMAT comparisons, you must first learn to spot them by learning certain key words or phrases that signal comparisons. Upon finding a comparison, you must identify the two things being compared and ensure that they are truly parallel, both with regard to structure and meaning.

Certain words and phrases signal comparisons. The chart shown to the right lists the most important of these signals. Whenever you see one of them, stop and find the two items being compared.

Comparison Signals	
like	as
unlike	as (adj.) as
likening	as many as
more than	as few as
greater than	as much as
less than	as little as
shorter than	as high as
different from*	as short as

*Note that the correct comparison is *different from*, not the commonly misused *different than.*

The word **like** is used to compare two nouns. The word **as** is used to compare two clauses.

"Like" vs. "As"

The words **like** and **as** are two of the most common comparison signals. Although they may seem interchangeable, for the purposes of the GMAT, they are not.

Like should be used to compare people or things (any nouns).

As should be used in a comparison involving clauses. A clause is any phrase that includes a verb. **As** can also be used in comparisons that use the construction **as . . . as**.

Incorrect: **Bella and June, AS their mother Stacy, are extremely smart.**
Correct:　 **Bella and June, LIKE their mother Stacy, are extremely smart.**

Incorrect: **Just LIKE swimming is good exercise, skiing is a great way to burn calories.**
Correct:　 **Just AS swimming is good exercise, skiing is a great way to burn calories.**

In the first example, simple nouns (**Bella and June** & **their mother Stacy**) are being compared, so *like* is required. In the second example, clauses with the verb **to be** are being compared, so *as* is required.

Note: **Like** is often misused in modern English. Do not use **like** when you mean **for example**. Instead, use the phrase **such as** (see page 18).

Manhattan GMAT Prep
the new standard

Keeping Comparisons Parallel

Comparisons must be logically parallel. That is, they must compare similar things.

> **Frank's build, like his brother, is extremely broad and muscular.**

Ask yourself: What two things are being compared? According to the sentence as written, **Frank's build** is being compared to **his brother**. This is not a logical comparison, because it does not compare similar things. In order to correct this error, we can change the comparison in one of two ways:

> **Frank, like his brother, has a broad and muscular build. OR**
> **Frank's build, like that of his brother, is extremely broad and muscular.**

These revisions both contain logical comparisons. The first compares **Frank** to **his brother**, while the second revision compares **Frank's build** to **that (the build) of his brother**.

Comparisons must be structurally parallel. That is, they must have a similar grammatical structure.

> **I enjoy flying by plane more than I like to drive in a car.**

Ask yourself: Are the objects of comparison grammatically parallel? No, because **enjoy flying by plane** does not have the same structure as **like to drive in a car**. In order to make the comparison structurally parallel, we can revise the sentence as follows:

> **I enjoy flying by plane more than driving by car.**

Here the phrase **flying by plane** parallels the phrase **driving by car**.

Comparative and Superlative Forms

When comparing two things, use the comparative form of an adjective or adverb. When comparing more than two things, use the superlative form of an adjective or adverb.

Irregular Forms

Adj./Adv.	Comparative	Superlative
Good	Better	Best
Bad	Worse	Worst
Much, Many	More	Most
Little	Little, less, lesser	Least
Far	Farther, further	Farthest, furthest

Regular Forms
Comparative: **She is SHORTER than her sister.** (Add -er)
Superlative: **She is the SHORTEST of her five siblings.** (Add -est)
Comparative: **You are MORE INTERESTING than she.** (Add the word **more**)
Superlative: **You are the MOST INTERESTING person here.** (Add the word **most**)

In the left margin:

When comparing only two things, use the comparative form. When comparing more than two things, use the superlative form.

Problem Set

In each of the following 15 sentences, circle all comparison signals and underline the items being compared. Then, rewrite each sentence ensuring that the items are logically and structurally similar.

1. As with other children in her neighborhood who were home-schooled, Joan sometimes missed being in a classroom with her peers.

2. In contrast to the trapeze artists who fumbled their routine, the antics of the circus clowns kept the audience entertained for hours.

3. The clothes hanging on the racks inside the store looked more appealing than in the store window.

4. There are about the equivalent number of gym members in the boxing class as in the aerobics class.

5. Brett decided to use his own money, but not his parents' credit card, to pay for the stereo.

6. Julia was able to climb the tree so fast as her brothers.

7. The blue dress looks more flattering on you than the red one.

8. Three times more students attended the prom this year than last year.

9. Joe went to bed early because his will to succeed in the race the following morning was greater than playing pool with his friends.

10. Sam was away on vacation longer than his friends.

11. Most of the audience did not enjoy the concert, likening it to grinding up metal.

12. Owning a car is still Dan's goal, like that of his parents when they were his age.

13. Covering the floors with tiles costs twice as much as linoleum.

14. Like a woman I once met on the bus, the hostess' attire was somewhat flamboyant.

15. The tycoon contributed more to the candidate's campaign than anyone else in the industry.

1. _Like_ other children in her neighborhood who were home-schooled, Joan sometimes missed being in a classroom with her peers.

2. _In contrast to_ the trapeze artists who fumbled their routine, the circus clowns kept the audience entertained for hours with their antics.

3. The clothes hanging on the racks inside the store looked _more appealing than_ those in the store window.

4. There are about _as many_ gym members in the boxing class _as_ there are in the aerobics class.

5. Brett decided to use his own money _rather than_ his parents' credit card to pay for the stereo.

6. Julia was able to climb the tree _as fast as_ her brothers did.

7. The blue dress looks _more flattering_ on you _than_ the red one does.

8. _Three times more_ students attended the prom this year _than_ did last year.

9. Joe went to bed early because his will to succeed in the race the following morning was _greater than_ his desire to play pool with his friends.

10. Sam was away on vacation _longer than_ his friends were.

11. Most of the audience did not enjoy the concert, _likening_ it _to_ the grinding of metal.

12. Owning a car is still Dan's goal, _as_ it was of his parents when they were his age.

13. Covering the floors with tiles costs _twice as much as_ covering them with linoleum.

14. _Like_ a woman I once met on the bus, the hostess was dressed somewhat flamboyantly.

15. The tycoon contributed _more_ to the candidate's campaign _than_ did anyone else in the industry.

Sentence Correction

Now that you have completed your study of COMPARISONS, it is time to test your skills on problems that have actually appeared on real GMAT exams over the past several years.

The problem set that follows is composed of past GMAT problems from two books published by GMAC (Graduate Management Admission Council):

The Official Guide for GMAT Review, 11th edition (pages 39-43 & 638-660)
The Official Guide for GMAT Verbal Review (pages 234-253)

The problems in the set below are primarily focused on COMPARISON issues. For each of these problems, identify the words, phrases, or clauses being compared. Eliminate answer choices that contain faulty comparisons, either logical or structural. Be sure to maintain parallelism and to use appropriate comparison words.

Note: Problem numbers preceded by "D" refer to questions in the Diagnostic Test chapter of *The Official Guide for GMAT Review, 11th edition* (pages 39-43).

Comparisons

11th edition: D35, D37, D47, D51, D52, 6, 10, 13, 23, 29, 37, 66, 68, 73, 77, 79, 85, 95, 96, 97, 99, 100, 103, 104, 122, 123, 128
Verbal Review: 10, 23, 31, 33, 36, 42, 45, 50, 68, 94, 98, 101, 106

g | Chapter 8
of
SENTENCE CORRECTION

IDIOMS

In This Chapter . . .

- Using Your Ear: Spot - Extract - Replace
- X Enough to Y vs. So X As to Y
- Idiom List

IDIOMS

Idioms are expressions that have unique forms. There is no hard and fast rule for determining the form of an idiom. In fact, it is this very uniqueness that makes an expression an idiom. For example: RANGE FROM X to Y is an idiomatic expression. Why is it **range from** and not **range between**? It just is. **Range from** is the accepted English convention, while **range between** is not.

Luckily for native English speakers, most idiomatic expressions are wired into your brain from years of hearing and speaking English. Your ear is your best weapon in choosing the correct idiomatic form for an expression.

For non-native speakers, the task is more difficult. However, the GMAT does tend to focus on certain common idioms. Memorizing these common idiomatic expressions can be very useful for evaluating many GMAT sentences.

The Spot - Extract - Replace Method will help you identify idiom errors.

Using Your Ear: Spot - Extract - Replace

Your ear is your most valuable weapon in trying to ascertain the proper form of a given idiom. However, you must understand how to use your ear in this regard.

A large percentage of New York City residents are native from other countries.

First, you must SPOT the suspect idiomatic expression. Repeat the sentence in your head until you spot what sounds like an idiom: **native from**.

Second, EXTRACT the idiom from the sentence and play with it in your head by inserting it into made-up sentences. In so doing, you will probably recognize that **native from** does not sound natural, but that **natives of** does.

Third, REPLACE the corrected idiom in the sentence and evaluate how it sounds.

A large percentage of New York City residents are NATIVES OF other countries.

Note that not every idiomatic expression is one indivisible unit. Often an idiomatic expression is split up within a sentence. Consider the following:

Not only is Mary tired, but she is hungry.

Here the suspect idiom that you spot is **not only . . . but**. By extracting it from the sentence, you will notice that this idiom is made up of two units (**not only** and **but**). You will also hear that the second half of the idiom is incomplete. The complete idiom should be **not only . . . but also**. We can revise the sentence accordingly:

Not only is Mary tired, but she is also hungry.

*Manhattan*GMAT*Prep

X Enough to Y vs. So X As to Y

There are some idiomatic expressions that are similar to one another but that do not mean the same thing. A classic example that sometimes appears on the GMAT is the difference between the two idiomatic expressions *X enough to Y* and *so X as to Y*.

The first expression is used when X is the criteria by which an ability to achieve Y is measured. For example:

Bob is tall **enough to** reach the top shelf.

In this sentence, height is the criteria by which the ability to reach the top shelf is measured. The focus here is Bob's *ability to reach the top shelf*.

The second expression is used when the characteristic X is so extreme in the particular case that Y results. For example:

Bob is **so** tall **as to** reach the top shelf.

In this sentence, Bob's height is so extreme that he actually can reach the top shelf. The focus here is the *consequence of Bob's extreme height*.

In order to know which expression to use, you must determine the focus of the sentence.

Similar idiomatic expressions do not necessarily convey the same meaning.

Idiom List

Review the following common idioms. This is not an exhaustive list, as there are thousands of idiomatic expressions in the English language. For native English speakers, it is unnecessary to spend time memorizing this list. You should spend most of your time perfecting the spot-extract-replace method, which helps your ear find idiomatic errors.

IDIOM LIST

a consequence of
a debate over
a responsibility to
a sequence of
able to X
access to
agree with (person/idea)
agree to (a plan or action)
allows for
appeal to
approve/disapprove of
an instance of
as a result of
as good as
as great as
as many . . . as
as much as
as X as to Y
ask X to Y
associate with
attend to
attribute X to Y
based on
be afraid of
believe X to be Y
better served by X than by Y
better than
both X and Y
capable of
centers on
claim to be
compare to (similarities)
compare with (differences)
concerned with
conform to
connection between X and Y
consider X Y (without 'to be')
contend that
contrast X with Y
credited with
declare X Y
declare Y X
defined as

demand that
dependent on
depends on whether
depicted as
determined by
differ from
different from
disagree with (person/idea)
discourage from
dispute whether
distinguish between X and Y
distinguish X from Y
doubt that
either X or Y
enable X to Y
encourage X to Y
enough X that Y
estimated to be
except for
expect to
fascinated by
forbid X to Y
identical with
in contrast to
in danger of
independent from
indifferent towards
insist that
interaction of
isolated from
just as X, so Y
know to do X
less X than Y
likely to be
mandate that
mistake X for Y
modeled after
more . . . than ever
more common among X than
    among Y
more X than Y
native to
a native of

neither X nor Y
no less . . . than
no less was X than was Y
not only X but also Y
not so much X as Y
not X but rather Y
noted that
permit X to Y
persuade X to Y
prefer X to Y
prohibit X from Y
potential to
range from X to Y
rates for (not 'of')
regard as
requiring that X Y
requiring X to Y
responsible for
resulting in
retroactive to
sacrifice X for Y
seem to indicate
similar to
so as not to be hindered by
so X as to (be) Y
so X as to constitute Y
so X that Y
subscribe to
such X as Y and Z
targeted at
the more X the greater Y
the same to X as to Y
to result in
to think of X as Y
used as
view X as Y
whether to
worried about (not 'over')
X enough to Y
X instead of Y
X is attributed to Y
X out of Y (numbers)
X regarded as Y

The expression **"consider to be"** is considered wordy on the GMAT. Use the verb **consider** without **"to be."**

Problem Set

In each of the following 15 sentences, underline all idiomatic expressions. For idioms that are split up, be sure to underline both parts. Use the spot-extract-replace method to determine whether each idiom is in its proper form. Then, rewrite each sentence using the corrected idiom.

1. Unaccustomed to being spontaneous, Jill couldn't decide whether she should be spending her bonus on a new computer.

2. The new mother spent most of the day worrying over her son's safety.

3. The reclusive playwright has been known as declining invitations to speak at college forums across the country.

4. Current office policy requires that all employees should submit vacation requests to their supervisors before taking those requests to the human resources department.

5. Someone who enrolls in an advanced dance class without prior experience is likely severely disadvantaged.

6. All the history professors considered the visiting lecturer as an expert in his field.

7. The success of the new restaurant depends on if it can appeal to a broad range of palates.

8. The sign in front of the Baker residence prohibits anyone to trespass on the property.

9. The chemical's potential was determined as a result of extensive research and experimentation.

10. The Pilgrims are credited as having celebrated the first Thanksgiving.

11. Jeff claims that he is the best quarterback his team has ever seen.

12. Although it was expected that Kelly would win the spelling bee, she stumbled on a fairly simple word.

13. The union demanded that its members should be receiving better pay.

14. Peter viewed babysitting his sister like a chore rather than a chance to become close to her.

15. Cheryl mistook the handsome boy's sudden appearance at her locker as a sign that the boy was interested in her.

1.   Unaccustomed to being spontaneous, Jill couldn't decide <u>whether to spend</u> her bonus on a new computer. *(whether to X)*

2.   The new mother spent most of the day <u>worrying about</u> her son's safety. *(worrying about X)*

3.   The reclusive playwright has been <u>known to decline</u> invitations to speak at college forums across the country. *(known to X)*

4.   Current office policy <u>requires that all employees submit</u> vacation requests to their supervisors before taking those requests to the human resources department. *(requires that X Y)* **OR** Current office policy <u>requires all employees to submit</u> vacation requests to their supervisors before taking those requests to the human resources department. *(requires X to Y)*

5.   Someone who enrolls in an advanced dance class without prior experience is <u>likely to be</u> at a severe disadvantage. *(likely to be)*

6.   All the history professors <u>considered the visiting lecturer an expert</u> in his field. *(consider X Y)*

7.   The success of the new restaurant <u>depends on whether</u> it can appeal to a broad range of palates. *(depends on whether)* OR <u>depends on its ability to appeal</u>... *(depends on X)*

8.   The sign in front of the Baker residence <u>prohibits anyone from trespassing</u> on the property. *(prohibits X from Y)* OR <u>prohibits trespassing</u>... *(prohibits X)*

9.   The chemical's potential was <u>determined by</u> extensive research and experimentation. *(determined by)*

10.   The Pilgrims are <u>credited with</u> having celebrated the first Thanksgiving. *(credited with)*

11.   Jeff <u>claims to be</u> the best quarterback his team has ever seen. *(claims to be)* OR <u>claims that he is</u>... *(claims that X)* (The original is grammatically correct as well.)

12.   Although Kelly <u>was expected to</u> win the spelling bee, she stumbled on a fairly simple word. *(expect to)*

13.   The union <u>demanded that its members receive better pay</u>. *(demanded that X Y)*

14.   Peter <u>viewed babysitting his sister as a chore</u> rather than a chance to become close to her. *(viewed X as Y)*

15.   Cheryl <u>mistook the handsome boy's sudden appearance at her locker for a sign</u> that the boy was interested in her. *(mistook X for Y)*

Sentence Correction

Now that you have completed your study of IDIOMS, it is time to test your skills on problems that have actually appeared on real GMAT exams over the past several years.

The problem set that follows is composed of past GMAT problems from two books published by GMAC (Graduate Management Admission Council):

The Official Guide for GMAT Review, 11th edition (pages 39-43 & 638-660)
The Official Guide for GMAT Verbal Review (pages 234-253)

The problems in the set below are primarily focused on IDIOM issues. For each of these problems, identify the idiom. Eliminate any answer choices that use an unidiomatic expression. Use your ear and the spot-extract-replace method to help you identify the correct form of the idiom.

Note: Problem numbers preceded by "D" refer to questions in the Diagnostic Test chapter of *The Official Guide for GMAT Review, 11th edition* (pages 39-43).

Idioms

11th edition: D45, 2, 16, 27, 30, 31, 40, 53, 55, 67, 82, 92, 121
Verbal Review: 9, 17, 20, 46, 48, 66, 76, 90, 108, 113

Chapter 9
of
SENTENCE CORRECTION

ODDS & ENDS

In This Chapter . . .

- Quantity
- Connecting Words
- Connecting Punctuation
- Things that are (Almost) Always Wrong

ODDS & ENDS

You now have many things to look for in analyzing a GMAT sentence. On a general level, look out for the three C's of sentence correction: Correctness, Concision, and Clarity. On a specific level, make sure to check each sentence for errors related to the following grammatical topics: (1) Subject-Verb Agreement, (2) Verb Tense, Mood, & Voice, (3) Pronouns, (4) Modifiers, (5) Parallelism, (6) Comparisons, and (7) Idioms.

The vast majority of GMAT grammar errors fall into one of the preceding categories. There are, however, a few other types of errors which may be found in GMAT sentences. If you have checked a sentence for all the major types of errors and you are still undecided between two sentence versions, consider the following odds & ends—additional grammar topics which may help you identify the correct sentence:

    (1)   Quantity
    (2)   Connecting Words and Punctuation
    (3)   Things That are Almost Always Wrong

> The word **many** modifies countable things. **Much** modifies uncountable things.

Quantity

In English, words and expressions of quantity are subject to strict grammatical rules. The GMAT tests your knowledge of these "quantity" rules.

<u>Rule #1: Words used for countable things VS. words used for uncountable things</u>

The following chart distinguishes between words and expressions that modify countable things and those that modify uncountable things:

Countable Modifiers	Uncountable Modifiers
Many hats	*Much* patience
As many hats *as* shirts	*As much* patience *as* kindness
Few/Fewer hats	*Little/Less* patience
Number of hats	*Amount* of patience

Countable items include **dollars**, **hats**, **buildings**, and **people**. Uncountable things include **money**, **water**, **wreckage**, and **patience**. If you are unsure as to whether something is countable or not, perform the counting test:

    For dollars: **1 dollar, 2 dollars, 3 dollars, and so forth.** This works; **dollar** is countable.
    For money: **1 money, 2 money, stop.** This does not work; **money** is uncountable.

Rule #2: Words used to relate two things VS. words used to relate three or more things

To relate two things, you must use different words from the words you use to relate three or more things. This chart highlights the most important words (the majority are a

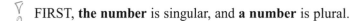

Relating 2 things	Relating 3 or more things
between X and Y	among X, Y, and Z
X is better than Y	X is the best (among X, Y, and Z)
X has more than Y	X has the most (among X, Y, and Z)
X has less than Y	X has the least (among X, Y, and Z)

review) that must be used when relating different numbers of things.

Remember, any answer choice containing the phrase **the numbers of** is incorrect.

Rule #3: **The number** or **number of** VS. **a number** or **the numbers of**

As you may recall from the Subject-Verb Agreement section, the word **number** is tricky depending on the expression in which it is used. There are two major points to remember:

FIRST, **the number** is singular, and **a number** is plural.

> **The number of dogs IS greater than the number of cats.**
> **A number of dogs ARE chasing away the cats.**

SECOND, **the numbers of** is incorrect. Stick to the expression **the number of**.

> Incorrect: **THE NUMBERS OF dogs in Montana are steadily increasing.**
> Correct: **THE NUMBER OF dogs in Montana is steadily increasing.**

Rule #4: Increase and decrease VS. greater and less

The words **increase** and **decrease** are NOT the same as the words **greater** and **less**. **Increase** and **decrease** express the change of ONE thing over time. **Greater** and **less** signal a comparison between TWO things.

> **The price of silver INCREASED by ten dollars.**
> **The price of silver is GREATER than the price of copper.**

Watch out for redundancy in sentences with the words **increase** and **decrease**.

> Incorrect: **The price of silver fell by a more than 35% decrease.**
> Correct: **The price of silver decreased by more than 35%.**

Decrease already includes the notion of falling or lowering, so the word **fell** is redundant. Similarly, **increase** includes the notion of **rising** or **growing**, so those words are redundant as well.

Connecting Words

In order for phrases and clauses to combine into a complete sentence, they must be connected together in the proper way by certain connecting words.

FIRST, watch out for sentences that have no logical connectors between two independent clauses. For example:

I need to relax, I have so many things to do!

This is termed a run-on sentence because it involves two independent sentences connected by nothing more than a comma (which is not enough!). It can be corrected by adding a logical "connecting" word such as **but**:

I need to relax, BUT I have so many things to do!

SECOND, make sure that clauses are connected by a logical "connecting" word:

She is not interested in playing sports, AND she likes watching them on TV.

The connecting word **and** is not logical because the two sentence parts are in opposition to each other. This can be corrected by choosing a different "connecting" word:

She is not interested in playing sports, BUT she likes watching them on TV.
OR
ALTHOUGH she is not interested in playing sports, she likes watching them on TV.

The following is a list of the most common connecting words:

and, or, nor, but, yet, although, when, because, for, since, before, after, if, unless

Be sure to choose a connector that logically fits into a given sentence.

Connecting words can help you avoid run-on sentences.

Connecting Punctuation

The two major punctuation marks that can connect sentence parts are the semicolon and the colon. The semicolon (;) is used to connect two closely related statements. BOTH statements must be able to stand alone as independent sentences.

>   Incorrect: **Andrew and Lisa are inseparable; doing everything together.**
>   Correct: **Andrew and Lisa are inseparable; they do everything together.**

In the first example, the second part of the sentence is incapable of standing on its own. Therefore, the two parts may NOT be connected by a semicolon. In the second example, the two sentence parts are both capable of standing alone. Therefore, they may be connected by a semicolon.

The colon (:) is used to equate two parts of a sentence. For example, it is often used to equate a list with its components. You should be able to insert the word **namely** after the colon. Only the statement that precedes the colon must be able to stand alone:

>   Incorrect: **I love listening to: classical, rock, and pop music.**
>   Correct: **I love many kinds of music: [namely] classical, rock, and pop.**

In the first example, the statement preceding the colon – **I love listening to** – cannot stand alone. In the second example, the statement preceding the colon can stand alone, and one can insert the word **namely** into the phrase following the colon.

Be sure not to confuse the semicolon (;) with the colon (:). The semicolon connects two independent clauses (each can stand on its own). The colon equates two parts of a sentence where the second part is dependent on the first part.

Things that are (Almost) Always Wrong

Finally, be aware that there are some words and phrases that appear on the GMAT that either always or almost always indicate incorrect answer choices. You should learn this list and be able to use the words and phrases shown below to identify wrong answers.

	INCORRECT	**CORRECT**
Do it	She asked him several times to take out the garbage, but she wasn't sure whether he would **do it**.	She asked him several times to take out the garbage, but she wasn't sure whether he would **do so**.
The numbers of	The politicians were amazed at **the numbers of** anti-war protesters.	The politicians were amazed at **the number of** anti-war protesters.
Whether or not	He couldn't decide **whether or not** to apply to Stanford.	He couldn't decide **whether** to apply to Stanford.

A semicolon is used only to connect two related complete sentences.

*Manhattan*GMAT*Prep
the new standard

Sentence Correction

Now that you have completed your study of ODDS & ENDS, it is time to test your skills on problems that have actually appeared on real GMAT exams over the past several years.

The problem set that follows is composed of past GMAT problems from two books published by GMAC (Graduate Management Admission Council):

The Official Guide for GMAT Review, 11th edition (pages 638-660)
The Official Guide for GMAT Verbal Review (pages 234-253)

The problems in the set below are primarily focused on ODDS & ENDS issues. For each of these problems, identify any errors relating to the odds & ends topics. Eliminate any answer choices that misuse expressions of quantity, connecting words, or connecting punctuation.

Odds & Ends
> *11th edition:* 4, 26, 51, 69, 87, 111
> *Verbal Review:* 5, 14, 60, 80, 92, 93, 111

Chapter 10
of
SENTENCE CORRECTION

OFFICIAL GUIDE
PROBLEM SET &
PROBLEM MATRIX

Sentence Correction

from *The Official Guide for GMAT Review, 11th edition* (pages 39-43 & 638-660) and *The Official Guide for GMAT Verbal Review* (pages 234-253)

The following is a REVIEW of all the Official Guide problem sets included in this guide. <u>Note</u>: Problem numbers preceded by "D" refer to questions in the Diagnostic Test chapter of *The Official Guide for GMAT Review, 11th edition* (pages 39-43).

Set 1: Complete after the THE 3 C's section.
11th edition: 8, 12, 14, 33, 36, 44, 80, 101, 118, 120, 124
Verbal Review: 2, 22, 26, 43, 54, 69, 75, 87, 105, 109

Set 2: Complete after the SUBJECT-VERB AGREEMENT section.
11th edition: D41, D43, 1, 3, 21, 34, 41, 42, 52, 61, 70, 90, 116, 131, 138
Verbal Review: 8, 16, 24, 34, 35, 44, 59, 74, 77, 102, 104

Set 3: Complete after the VERB TENSE, MOOD, & VOICE section.
11th edition: D39, 15, 28, 57, 58, 59, 62, 63, 74, 75, 76, 81, 83, 94, 108, 126, 137
Verbal Review: 3, 13, 21, 28, 30, 37, 40, 65, 83, 86, 95, 103

Set 4: Complete after the PRONOUNS section.
11th edition: D42, 5, 25, 32, 43, 89, 127, 130, 133
Verbal Review: 12, 15, 19, 29, 41, 49, 53, 55, 58, 61, 67, 71, 72, 73, 85, 89

Set 5: Complete after the MODIFIERS section.
11th edition: D40, D44, D49, 7, 20, 24, 38, 45, 50, 71, 72, 78, 93, 98, 102, 105, 107, 109, 110, 114, 125, 135
Verbal Review: 7, 18, 32, 38, 39, 57, 63, 78, 79, 84, 88, 91, 96, 107, 110, 112

Set 6: Complete after the PARALLELISM section.
11th edition: D36, D38, D46, D48, D50, 9, 11, 17, 18, 19, 22, 35, 39, 46, 47, 48, 49, 54, 56, 60, 64, 65, 84, 86, 88, 91, 106, 112, 113, 115, 117, 119, 129, 132, 134, 136
Verbal Review: 1, 4, 6, 11, 25, 27, 47, 51, 52, 56, 62, 64, 70, 81, 82, 97, 99, 100

Set 7: Complete after the COMPARISONS section.
11th edition: D35, D37, D47, D51, D52, 6, 10, 13, 23, 29, 37, 66, 68, 73, 77, 79, 85, 95, 96, 97, 99, 100, 103, 104, 122, 123, 128
Verbal Review: 10, 23, 31, 33, 36, 42, 45, 50, 68, 94, 98, 101, 106

Set 8: Complete after the IDIOMS section.
11th edition: D45, 2, 16, 27, 30, 31, 40, 53, 55, 67, 82, 92, 121
Verbal Review: 9, 17, 20, 46, 48, 66, 76, 90, 108, 113

Set 9: Complete after the ODDS & ENDS section.
11th edition: 4, 26, 51, 69, 87, 111
Verbal Review: 5, 14, 60, 80, 92, 93, 111

OFFICIAL GUIDE
PROBLEM MATRIX

The following pages contain a MATRIX that identifies the grammatical topics tested by each Sentence Correction question in *The Official Guide for GMAT Review, 11th edition* (pages 39-43 & 638-660) and *The Official Guide for GMAT Verbal Review* (pages 234-253).

Use this MATRIX to complete the following exercise:

(1) Review each Sentence Correction question and find all of the grammatical problems in both the original sentence AND each of the answer choices.

(2) Use the MATRIX to check whether you have correctly identified all of the grammatical issues tested by each question.

The following matrix refers to Sentence Correction questions in *The Official Guide for GMAT Review, 11th edition* (pages 39-43 & 638-660). Note: Problem numbers preceded by "D" refer to questions in the Diagnostic Test chapter (pages 39-43).

#	Concision & Clarity	Subj-Verb Agreement	Verb Tense/Voice/Mood	Pronouns	Modifiers
D35					modifying clause
D36	wordiness, fragment			missing antecedents	
D37	wordiness, fragment				
D38	wordiness				'that' modifier clause
D39			tense		
D40	run-on sentence			ambiguous antecedents	modifying phrases
D41		'discovery' is singular		illogical antecedent	'that' modifier clause
D42	wordiness		tense	ambiguous antecedents	
D43	wordiness	'proportion' is singular			modifier with relative pronoun
D44	sentence fragment			missing antecedent	modifying phrases
D45	sentence fragment		passive voice		modifying clause
D46			tense		adverb vs. adjective
D47					
D48					
D49			tense		misplaced modifiers
D50				ambiguous antecedents	
D51	wordiness		passive voice		
D52	wordiness				
1	wordiness	'surge' is singular			
2	wordiness		tense		
3	clarity: word placement	'Diabetes' is singular	tense		
4					
5	redundancy			agreement in number	
6	wordiness				
7			tense		essential vs. non-essential
8	wordiness	'inventories' is plural			adverb vs. adjective
9					'which' modifier clause
10					
11					
12	redundancy, wordiness				adverb vs. adjective
13					
14	double negative				
15	sentence fragment		tense		
16					
17					
18	run-on sentence				incorrect modifier
19	redundancy, wordiness				
20				missing antecedent	modifier touches modified noun
21		'fragments' is plural			
22					

#	Parallelism	Comparisons	Idioms	Odds & Ends
D35	clauses	parallel comparison		
D36	subjects, phrasing		'for every X, Y'	
D37	noun phrases	parallel comparison		
D38	prepositional phrases			
D39		'more than likely'	'probably not X, but more than likely Y'	
D40	modifying phrases			
D41	noun phrases			
D42				
D43				
D44	modifying phrases			use of 'but'
D45			'declares Y X'	
D46	clauses			
D47		parallel comparison	'the ability to'	
D48	modifying phrases		'more X than Y'	
D49				
D50	verb phrases			
D51	nouns	parallel comparison		
D52	clauses	parallel comparison, 'like' vs. 'as'	'just as X, so Y'	
1				
2			'X is more than Y'	
3				
4		parallel comparison		quantity: 'much' vs. 'many'
5				
6		parallel comparison, 'like' vs. 'as'		
7				
8				'when' vs. 'if'
9	verb phrases			'although' vs. 'but'
10		parallel comparison	'reluctant to'	
11	verb phrases			
12				'after' vs. 'following'
13		superlative form		'since' vs. 'after'
14				'or' vs. 'and'
15				'although' vs. 'but'
16		parallel comparison	'unlike X, Y'	
17	verb phrases			
18	clauses			
19	verbs of being			
20				
21			'estimated to be'	
22	verb phrases in a list			

#	Concision & Clarity	Subj-Verb Agreement	Verb Tense/Voice/Mood	Pronouns	Modifiers
23					
24					participle modifier
25	wordiness			missing antecedent, agreement	
26					
27	wordiness				
28			'if' vs. 'whether'		
29				agreement in number	
30					
31					
32				possessive poison	
33	wordiness				
34	wordiness	'efforts' is plural			
35					
36	clarity of meaning				
37					
38					adjective vs. adverb
39					
40				incorrect antecedents	
41		'are' is plural			
42		missing verb for subject			
43	wordiness			missing antecedent	
44	wordiness				
45	wordiness		tense, passive voice		'that' modifier clause
46	redundancy, wordiness				
47					
48	redundancy, wordiness				
49	redundancy, wordiness	'programs' is plural			essential vs. non-essential
50	wordiness				'that' modifier clause
51	wordiness			ambiguous antecedent	
52	sentence fragment	compound subject is plural		agreement in number	
53					
54	wordiness		passive voice		
55					
56					
57	wordiness		conditional	ambiguous antecedents	
58			tense		use of 'that'
59	redundancy, word placement		tense		
60					adjective vs. adverb
61		'enrollments' is plural		agreement in number	
62			tense		

#	Parallelism	Comparisons	Idioms	Odds & Ends
23		comparative vs. superlative	'difficulty to X'	
24				
25				
26			'the same to X as to Y'	use of semicolon; articles
27			'in danger of X'	
28			'ability to X'	
29		'like' vs. 'as'		
30			'as much as', 'not so much as'	
31			'credit X with Y'	
32			'X is expected to Y'	
33				
34				
35	adjective phrases			
36				
37		'as' vs. 'than'		
38				
39	verb phrases			
40			'between X & Y'	
41				
42				
43				
44			'from X to Y'	
45	verb phrases			
46	clauses			
47	adverbial phrases, 'and' in series			
48	verb phrases		'recommend that X Y'	
49	verb phrases			
50				
51				'for' vs. 'in that'
52				
53			'requires X to Y'	
54	verb phrases		'will try to', 'restrictions on'	
55	verb phrases		'not only X but also Y'	
56	participial phrases, modifying clauses		'act as'	
57				
58			'doubt that'	
59				
60	verb phrases		'as a means to'	
61	verb forms			
62			'allowed to'	

#	Concision & Clarity	Subj-Verb Agreement	Verb Tense/Voice/Mood	Pronouns	Modifiers
63			tense, 'whether' vs. 'if'	ambiguous/illogical anteced.	
64	wordiness		infinitive		essential vs. non-essential
65				'citrus' & 'fruit' are singular	
66					
67					dangling modifier
68			tense		
69		'dioxins' is plural			
70		'it' is singular			
71					antecedent of 'which' modifier
72			passive voice		modifier touches modified noun
73					
74	sentence fragment		verb tense		
75			tense		
76			tense		
77	redundancy	'costs' is plural			
78			tense		misplaced modifier
79			tense		
80	wordiness, clarity of meaning				
81			tense		
82					
83			subjunctive mood		
84				missing antecedents	
85					
86			passive voice		
87				missing antecedent	
88					
89				relative pronouns	
90		'pattern' is singular			
91					
92	clarity: known/unknown			agreement in number	
93					unclear modifiers
94			'if' vs. 'whether'		
95					
96					
97	wordiness, redundancy				misplaced modifying phrase
98	wordiness, redundancy			ambiguous antecedent	modifier with relative pronoun
99					
100	wordiness				
101	sentence fragment		tense		incorrect modifier: 'where'
102				ambiguous antecedent	misplaced mod., relative clause

#	Parallelism	Comparisons	Idioms	Odds & Ends
63			purpose is expressed by 'to'	
64	nouns, 'is' vs. 'refers to'			
65	parallel infinitives			
66	verb forms	parallelism (logic & agreement)		
67			'attribute X to Y'; 'X is attributed to Y'	
68		illogical comparison	'admit to X'	
69				'much' vs. 'many'
70				comma vs. '&'
71			'known to X'	
72				
73	verb phrases	'like' vs. 'as'		
74				
75				
76			'as many X as Y'	
77		'less' vs. 'lower'		
78				
79		'like' vs. 'as'	'using X as Y'	
80				
81				
82			'require X to Y'	
83				
84	infinitives			
85		illogical comparison		
86	verb phrases			
87			'not X, but rather Y'	semicolon
88	verb phrases			
89				
90				
91	verb phrases			
92			'X ordered that Y be Z'ed'	
93				
94				
95		illogical comparison		
96		illogical comparison		
97	clauses	parallel comparison, 'like' vs. 'as'		
98				countable modifier
99	clauses	parallel comparison	'just as X, so Y'	
100		parallel comparison		
101			purpose is expressed by 'to'	
102				

#	Concision & Clarity	Subj-Verb Agreement	Verb Tense/Voice/Mood	Pronouns	Modifiers
103					'which' modifier clause
104	wordiness				
105	wordiness				misplaced mod., relative clause
106					
107					'which' modifier clause
108			'if' vs. 'whether'		
109					dangling modifier
110					need a comma for modifier
111	wordiness			ambiguous antecedent	
112	redundancy				
113					
114	wordiness				essential vs. non-essential
115					
116		'fascination' is singular	tense		
117					
118	wordiness				
119					
120	redundancy				
121					
122					
123				agreement in number	
124	wordy, clarity: known/unknown		tense		
125					misplaced modifier
126			conditional		
127				agreement in number	
128					
129			passive voice		
130				relative pronouns	
131	wordiness	'words' is plural			
132					
133				agreement, logic	
134					
135					dangling modifier
136					
137			tense		
138		agreement errors			

#	Parallelism	Comparisons	Idioms	Odds & Ends
103		parallel comparison		
104	participial phrases	'like' vs. 'as'	'rather than'	
105				
106	verb phrases		'either X or Y'	
107			distinguishes between 'X & Y'	
108			'whether to X'	
109				
110				
111				use of semicolon
112	noun phrases with 'both'			
113	verb phrases			
114				
115	infinitives		'consider X Y'	
116				
117	noun phrases			
118				
119	noun phrases			
120				
121			'claims to X'	
122		'like' vs. 'as'		
123		parallel comparison		
124				
125		'like' vs. 'as'		
126				'more than' vs. 'greater than'
127	verb phrases			
128		'many' vs. 'much'		
129	verb phrases			
130	clauses			
131				
132	noun phrases			
133				
134	noun phrases			
135				
136	verb phrases			
137	elements separated by conjunction			
138				

The following matrix refers to Sentence Correction questions in *The Official Guide for GMAT Verbal Review* (pages 234-253).

#	Concision & Clarity	Subj-Verb Agreement	Verb Tense/Voice/Mood	Pronouns	Modifiers
1					
2	clarity: known/unknown, run-on				'that' modifier clause
3			tense	'which' vs. 'who'	
4			passive, inconsis. tense		
5	redundancy		passive voice		
6				missing antecedent	
7	wordiness		passive voice		dangling modifier
8	sentence fragment	'costs' is plural			
9					
10					
11		compound subject is plural			
12				agreement in number	
13	wordiness		tense		
14					
15				agreement in number	
16	wordiness	'values' is plural	passive voice		
17					
18					meaning
19				multiple issues	
20			passive voice	agreement in number	
21			tense		
22	wordiness, clarity of meaning		passive voice		
23					
24		2 singular subjects			
25					
26	clarity: multiple meanings				
27					
28			tense		
29	clarity of meaning			ambiguous antecedents	
30		compound subject is plural	tense		
31					
32				agreement with anteced.	'that occurred' vs. 'occurring'
33					adjective vs. adverb
34	wordiness	'equipment' is singular			
35	clarity: known/unknown	'rise' is singular	tense		
36					
37			tense		
38					dangling modifier
39			tense, conditional		adjective vs. adverb
40			tense		

#	Parallelism	Comparisons	Idioms	Odds & Ends
1	verb phrases in a list			
2	clauses			
3				
4	prepositional phrases			
5				'numbers of' is always wrong
6	noun phrases in a list			
7				
8				
9			'range from X to Y'	
10		'like' vs. 'as'	'X as an instance of Y'	
11	clauses			
12				
13				
14			'between X & Y'	'between' vs. 'among'
15				
16				
17			'mistake X for Y'	
18				
19				
20			'think of X as Y'	
21				
22	parallelism of 'partly'			
23		'like' vs. 'as,' logic		
24				
25	verb phrases			
26				
27	clauses			
28				
29				
30				
31		'like' vs. 'as,' logic		
32				
33		'as old as' vs. 'older than'		
34				
35				
36		parallelism	'no less X than Y'	
37				
38				
39				
40			'elect to X'	

#	Concision & Clarity	Subj-Verb Agreement	Verb Tense/Voice/Mood	Pronouns	Modifiers
41	clarity: known/unknown			agreement	
42					
43	wordiness				
44		'term' is singular	tense		
45					
46	sentence fragment		passive voice		
47					
48					
49			tense	agreement in number	
50					
51					
52					
53	wordiness			ambiguous antecedent	
54	wordiness				
55				relative pronouns	
56					
57	wordiness				dangling modifier
58	wordiness			ambiguous antecedent	
59		agreement, logic & number			
60				missing antecedent	
61	wordiness, clarity of meaning			missing pronoun	
62					
63					dangling & misplaced mod.
64				missing antecedent	
65			tense	'it' vs. 'so'	
66					
67				missing antecedent	
68		multiple agreement errors			
69	wordiness, clarity of meaning			missing antecedent	
70					
71				ambiguous antecedents	
72				agreement in number	
73					misplaced modifier
74				'bank' is singular	
75	wordiness				
76	redundancy				
77		'each' & 'every one' are sing.			
78	clarity: word placement		conditional		adjective vs. adverb
79					antecedent of 'which' mod.
80	sentence fragment		tense		

#	Parallelism	Comparisons	Idioms	Odds & Ends
41			'requires X to Y'	
42		illogical comparison		
43				
44				
45	verb phrases	illogical comparison		
46			'not only X but also Y'	
47	clauses		'more X than ever'	
48			'prohibit X from Y'	
49				
50		illogical comparison		
51	noun phrases			
52	verb phrases		'not only X but also Y'	
53			'restitution for X'	
54	noun phrases		'both X & Y'	
55				
56	noun phrases			
57				
58				
59				
60			'not X, but rather Y'	semicolon
61				
62	infinitives			
63				
64	adjective phrases			
65				
66	verb phrases		'not only X but also Y'	
67	noun phrases			
68		illogical comparison		
69				
70	infinitives			
71	verb phrases			
72				
73				
74				
75				
76			'rates for (prices)'	
77				
78				
79				
80				

#	Concision & Clarity	Subj-Verb Agreement	Verb Tense/Voice/Mood	Pronouns	Modifiers
81	wordiness				
82					
83			conditional, tense		
84					antecedent of 'which' mod.
85	redundancy			missing antecedent	
86			tense	missing antecedent	
87	clarity: multiple meanings				
88					'little' vs. 'few'
89				agreement in number	
90	clarity: known/unknown				
91					misplaced modifier
92					
93	run-on sentence				
94					
95			conditional		
96					possessive poison, meaning
97					
98					
99					
100	wordiness				
101					
102			tense	'army' is singular	
103			tense		
104		'papers' is plural	tense		
105	wordiness, clarity: such as/like		tense		
106					
107					misplaced mod.; use of 'that'
108					
109	wordiness, redundancy				
110	wordiness				misplaced modifier
111					
112					misplaced modifier
113					

#	Parallelism	Comparisons	Idioms	Odds & Ends
81	noun phrases			
82	verb phrases			
83				
84	verb phrases		'either X or Y'	
85				
86			'allow X to be Y'	
87				
88				
89			'better served by X than by Y'	
90			'ordered X to Y'	
91			'substitute X for Y'	
92				'as many as' vs. 'equivalent to'
93				
94		parallel comparison		
95			'connection between X & Y'	
96				
97	noun phrases			
98		parallel comparison		
99	verb phrases			
100	verb phrases			
101		parallel comparison		
102				
103				
104	noun phrases			
105		'like' vs. 'such as'		
106		ambiguous comparison		
107				
108			'not only X but also Y'	
109				
110				
111				semicolon
112				
113			'as a result of'	

To waive "Finance I" at Harvard Business School you must:

    (A) Be a CFA

    (B) Have prior coursework in finance

    (C) Have two years of relevant work experience in the financial sector

    (D) Pass a waiver exam

    (E) None of the above; one cannot waive core courses at HBS

What are the requirements of an Entrepreneurial Management major at the Wharton School?

    (1) Completion of 5 credit units (cu) that qualify for the major

    (2) Participation in the Wharton Business Plan Competition during the 2nd year of the MBA program

(A) Statement (1) ALONE is sufficient, but statement (2) alone is not sufficient.

(B) Statement (2) ALONE is sufficient, but statement (1) alone is not sufficient.

(C) BOTH statements TOGETHER are sufficient, but NEITHER statement ALONE is sufficient.

(D) EACH statement ALONE is sufficient.

(E) Statements (1) and (2) TOGETHER are NOT sufficient.

Once You Ace the GMAT, Get Ready to Ace Your Applications!

To make an informed decision in applying to a school—and to craft an effective application that demonstrates an appreciation of a program's unique merits—**it's crucial that you do your homework**. Clear Admit School Guides cut through the gloss of marketing materials to give you the hard facts about a program, and then put these school-specific details in context so you can see how programs compare. In the guides, you'll find detailed, comparative information on vital topics such as:

- The core curriculum and first-year experience
- Leading professors in key fields
- Student clubs and conferences
- Full-time job placement by industry and location
- Student demographics
- International and experiential learning programs
- Tuition, financial aid and scholarships
- Admissions deadlines and procedures

Now available for top schools including:
Chicago, Columbia, Harvard, Kellogg, MIT, Stanford, Tuck and Wharton

A time-saving source of comprehensive information, Clear Admit School Guides have been featured in *The Economist* and lauded by applicants, business school students and MBA graduates:

"Purchasing the Clear Admit HBS School Guide was one of best decisions I made. I visited HBS three times and have every book and pamphlet that covers the top business schools, but nothing can compare to the Clear Admit guides in offering up-to-date information on every aspect of the school's academic and social life that is not readily available on the school's website and brochures. Reading a Clear Admit School Guide gives an applicant the necessary, detailed school information to be competitive in the application process."
—An applicant to Harvard

"I want to tip my hat to the team at Clear Admit that put these guides together. I'm a recent graduate of Wharton's MBA program and remain active in the admissions process (serving as an alumni interviewer to evaluate applicants). I can't tell you how important it is for applicants to show genuine enthusiasm for Wharton and I think the Clear Admit School Guide for Wharton captures many of the important details, as well as the spirit of the school. **This sort of information is a must for the serious MBA applicant.**"
—A Wharton MBA graduate

Question #1: (e) and Question #2 (a)